HELP! I'M A
FACEBOOKAHOLIC

HELP! I'M A FACEBOOKAHOLIC

INSIDE THE CRAZY WORLD OF SOCIAL NETWORKING

TANYA COOKE

JOHN BLAKE

Published by John Blake Publishing Ltd,
3 Bramber Court, 2 Bramber Road,
London W14 9PB, England

www.johnblakepublishing.co.uk

First published in paperback in 2011

ISBN: 978 1 84358 334 9

British Library Cataloguing-in-Publication Data:

A catalogue record for this book is available from the British Library.

Design by www.envydesign.co.uk

Printed in Great Britain by CPI Bookmarque, Croydon CRO 4TD

1 3 5 7 9 10 8 6 4 2

Papers used by John Blake Publishing are natural, recyclable products
made from wood grown in sustainable forests. The manufacturing processes
conform to the environmental regulations of the country of origin.

ACKNOWLEDGEMENTS

I would like to thank everyone who contributed to this book, particularly my wonderful researcher Jessie McLaughlin and my good friend Jacky Hyams without whose help I would be a gibbering wreck. I would also like to thank Lizzie Heathcote and Bridget Freer for their input, and all the people who shared their personal experiences no matter how embarrassing. Finally, I'd like to say a big thank you to my three children for their unstinting willingness to engage in first-hand social-networking research for hours… and hours… and hours… Er, you can turn it off now, guys!

CONTENTS

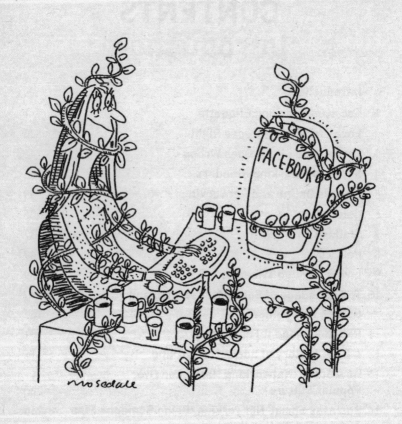

moscatelli

Introduction

L ike cars and mobile phones, social-networking is one of those phenomena that have become so deeply ingrained so quickly that it's impossible to imagine what we did without them.

As well as being useful in a practical sense, social-networking satisfies all the basic human emotional needs – communication, continuity, support. What could be more utopian than an instantly accessible online community of interconnecting networks not limited by barriers of geography or finance or social class?

From the moment it first hit the mainstream, social-networking became the Brave New World. Through it, anyone, anywhere could gain access to information, friendship groups or even their favourite celebrities without having to put their hands in their pockets or even leave the house. No wonder we all signed up in our droves. First CompuServe and AOL, then MySpace, Friends Reunited and now Facebook and Twitter – all of them offering that holy grail of membership to an egalitarian, yet seemingly exclusive club.

And our appetite has shown no sign of abating.

Figures from July 2010, show that 500 million people are now signed up to that Daddy of all social-networking sites, Facebook, sharing more than three billion pictures every month and sixty million status updates a day. At last count, Twitter was boasting 145 million registered users.

A 2010 study by online PR and social media firm Simply Zesty, showed that 30 million UK residents have visited at least one social-networking site in the last four weeks and we spend an average of just over six hours a month on social media forums. Sixty-four per cent of us have our own profiles on a social network.

Quite simply, social-networking has become an integral part of the landscape of our lives.

Of course, as with any new and overwhelmingly popular phenomenon, the backlash hasn't been far behind. As social-networking has increasingly become a fixture in family lives, we worry about the effect on children, on relationships, on friendships. Divorce lawyers have warned of the dangers of hooking up with exes online, psychologists are concerned about the devaluation of friendship. As the social-networking bug has spread to the workplace, there have been questions raised about how much time employees are spending online, and how much they are inadvertently giving away to future employers.

The result is that many of us now maintain a love-hate relationship with social-networking. We're addicted to it, in the sense that checking our profiles is often the first thing we do in the morning and the last thing we do at night. Now that we can access our favourite sites from our phones, we update from the bus, from the toilet, even from the altar. We join political groups on it, we raise money on it, we share videos and photographs on it. We can't get enough of it, and yet at the same time, it scares us.

The facility to connect with the past, so we never quite leave anything, or anyone, behind, the window onto other people's lives, the feeling that everything we do is somehow on show – these things can all leave us feeling as if our lives no longer completely belong to us, that nothing is entirely private.

The sheer scale of the networks, the idea that every person and every page is another link in a never-ending chain of interconnecting links, can sometimes be overwhelming. Once we start, where on earth do we stop? Social networks offer to put the individual in touch with the world, but how do we, with our limited time and energies, handle those limitless possibilities without losing our way? And how do we achieve a balance so that our virtual lives don't end up detracting from our real ones?

There is no sphere of our lives that hasn't been affected by social-networking. Love, work, friendship, politics, music, language – sites like Facebook have infiltrated them all. Social-networking has influenced the way we interact with our children, the way we find romantic partners, the way we throw parties or stage exhibitions. It has forced us to re-evaluate the nature of celebrity, and of obsession and popular culture. It has changed how we do business, how we make friends and even how we care for our pets.

We cannot escape it. And yet we do not quite understand it.

With the online world changing every day, and social media changing right along with it, no one can ever claim to fully comprehend the possibilities of social-networking, nor be fully aware of its limitations.

This book certainly doesn't pretend to be a comprehensive guide through the uncharted maze that is social-networking, but it will give you an insight into how it has changed the everyday landscape of our lives, and some of the ways in which we can gain from this new virtual world, without losing sight of what's important in the real one.

As social-networking inveigles its way into the heart of everything we do and the debate rages about whether it's a wonderful tool for uniting individuals, or a sinister force by which big business can take over our lives, it's easy to lose sight of the fact that social-networking, above all things, is supposed to be fun.

So let's lighten up, and log on. The ride is just beginning.

'I told you never to phone, tweet, poke or superpoke me at work.'

1

Social-Networking Etiquette

Life was hard enough when all you had to worry about was how to tell if the guy at the bar fancied you, or whether a suit jacket with jeans would leave you feeling under-dressed. Social-networking has brought with it a whole new dimension of etiquette problems. What status update to post? How often to update it? Do you put up photos of a party that not everyone was invited to? How do you deal with a friend request from someone you just can't abide?

The new rules of social-networking are a minefield and because technology is constantly evolving, they are always in a state of flux. No wonder so many of us feel like we're stumbling from one online faux pas to another.

One of the problems of social-networking is the it combines that casual informality of a coffee morning chat or a pub meet-up with the permanence of the written word. So while you can get up in the morning and delete the drunken message you found so hysterical the night before, you can't stop other people from having seen it or forwarding it on to all their mates. And once something is printed in black and white, you can't tell people they misheard, or misunderstood or even flat out deny it.

Another troubling feature is the fear that our social-networking profiles will come to define us to other people, so we invest a disproportionate amount of energy and anxiety in worrying about the image we're portraying. Without cheating (there exist applications such as Pimp My Profile for those suffering from extreme Profile Inadequacy Syndrome), we worry that our picture might not be attractive enough, our updates not witty enough, our friends not gushing enough to give out the right impression.

So it's essential to master the rudimentary rules of social-networking etiquette…

RULE ONE: Choose Your Profile Pic Wisely

You might think that choosing a photo to adorn your profile page is a question of just uploading the first picture to hand that (preferably) doesn't show you with three chins or looking like your eyes have been stolen. Well, you'd be wrong. Your profile picture is the first thing people look at when they navigate to your page, and like it or not they're going to make snap judgements about you depending on what they see. Don't want to be instantly pigeonholed? Well, make sure you avoid the stereotypical photo giveaways.

The Party Animal: Your photo will show you surrounded by mates, probably in the vicinity of a watering-hole of some kind, and almost certainly holding some sort of alcoholic beverage. You will be at the centre of the group, quite possibly striking a ridiculous pose, and almost definitely wearing a comedy hat. What you are saying to anyone who comes across your page is 'I'm popular, I'm fun and I already have tons of friends, which is why you will desperately want to join my list in the hope that you'll be invited to some of the fun parties I go to all the time, just like this one!'

The Eccentric: Your photo will be a starfish, or a fried egg, or perhaps your own knee made up to look like a face. This will tell people that you are a) not interested in personal vanity, b) a quirky individual who refuses to be pigeonholed and/or c) deeply insecure about your looks.

The Narcissist: Your photo will feature a close-up of you (naturally), probably taken by you (naturally) on a mobile phone in the privacy of your own home so that no one else sees the amount of preparation that goes into giving your hair that casual messy look. You will be pouting, of course, and you'll be holding the camera at arm's length slightly above you, so there's no hint of a double chin (but more than a hint of cheeky cleavage). Your pose will immediately let people know that not only are you drop-dead gorgeous, but you actually have 'attitude'. All right?

The Adventurer: Standing on top of a rugged hillside, silhouetted against the blue sky, you'll have your arms outstretched and a radiant smile on your glowing, weather-tinted face. Or maybe you'll be in a canoe, holding a paddle aloft having just finished rowing the length of the Amazon. Or you might be halfway down a mountainside, your skis perfectly aligned and your tanned face in sharp contrast to the white of the snow and of your own teeth as you flash a blinding smile. Whatever action pose your photo captures, it will be sending out a very clear message: 'I believe life is for living. I might have a social-networking page, but don't expect me to check it very often as I have far better uses for my time.'

The Mid-Lifer: The photo will have been taken around twenty-five years ago and will feature a very young, ridiculously fresh-faced version of you, probably taken at university and wearing clothes from Oxfam in a stylish and individual way. It might even be in black and white. 'I could have put a recent picture of me up here – maybe that one standing next to my adult son with my receding hairline clearly on show. But that isn't the real me! I want people to see that inside the sad shell in the M&S raincoat and magnifying specs, there beats the heart of the cool young dude with the interesting asymmetric hairstyle and size 30 waist. That's why I've also listed on my profile page all fifty-five of my favourite albums from the 1980s!'

The Comedian: There you are dressed up as a giant chicken, or sporting a false moustache. Or maybe it's a picture of your favourite cartoon character – Bart Simpson, or Kenny from *South Park*. Whatever photo you choose, it SHOUTS 'I'm wacky and crazy, me, never a dull moment when I'm around!' What you're hoping is that people will see your zany photo and want to be your friend in the belief that you'll always keep them entertained and laughing – which is a cert once they find you can recite entire episodes of *The Office* from memory!

How to improve your Facebook photo

If you're starting to worry that you might be sending out the wrong messages with your photo, don't despair. Here's some advice on improving your Facebook image from body language and behavioural expert, Judi James:

'Choosing your Facebook photo is about projecting your image in a positive way, so you have to start by thinking about exactly how you want to be seen by a large number of people, including people who may be linked to your working life or career.

'You probably want to appear natural and normal, but you do have to bear in mind the fact that portraying yourself in a sexual way might not be very helpful in your working life, i.e. when it comes to getting a promotion, or if you're looking for a first job.

'We might not be conscious of it, but there is a psychological "slant" to any photo we select of ourselves to define the essence of "me". There's nothing new in this: Henry VIII chose portraits of himself that showed him as strong, virile and physical in order to intimidate his enemies and seduce women.

'And his daughter, Elizabeth I used her image as "spin" in portraits an equally powerful way: the message she gave out in her images was "Yes, I might be a woman, but I'm strong. And I'm fertile." (No one knows for sure if she was The Virgin Queen, anyway.)

'Even now, politicians will use carefully chosen images of themselves to project the right message: casual body language, sleeves rolled up, a very visible hand wearing a wedding ring. The message here? "I'm a regular, normal guy, someone loves me and I can have kids".

'So your choice of photo, ideally, should aim for a shot that says as much as possible about you – but only the things that you want to say! Remember that when you are looking at the photo, you see the story behind it, but others won't, so be conscious of how it looks at face value. Avoid irony too. Some over-posed shots might be intended to be ironic, but any new contacts are more likely to think you're taking yourself far too seriously.'

If you really want to impress with your photo, Judi advises:

- PORTRAITS are good, but beware of coming across as vain or arrogant. Natural looking shots work best – but with a certain amount of modesty.
- HOLIDAY snaps can wind up looking smug or a bit naïve: 'Ooh look at me, I'm rich enough to travel'.
- PARTY shots in a group might, you think, show you to be outgoing and bubbly. But the message is more likely to come across as 'I have friends and we drink'.
- CHILDHOOD shots can look like a bid to show your more fragile or naughty self. In a way, with this type of photo you're apologising in advance for any spontaneous, tactless comments.
- SEXY shots, as we've already seen, can give the wrong message, in fact they can appear rather sad, especially as they'll be seen by a lot of people. So a sexy shot can just look like a sad advert: 'Ooh I'm up for it, me!'
- FUNNY photos can work sometimes, but, sadly, they can also be the signature of someone with no real sense of humour; dull people are desperate to prove how entertaining they are.
- KINKY photos, such as wearing dominatrix fancy dress are pseudo aggressive, aimed at stopping people in their tracks by

shouting, 'Hey! Don't mess with me!' Such photos are often confusing as they are rarely used by really angry people. So using such a shot could give out the message that your niceness is all a show.

- CELEBRITY photos can look like a bit of a 'mask', hinting that while others might be up for an open, friendly conversation, you'll be at your own masked ball, playing your cards very close to your chest.
- PETS look cute. But using a puppy as a front for your persona can be a modesty 'joke' that is too much of a cliché.

The ideal Facebook shot, according to Judi is:

1 Black and white – it looks stylish and cool.
2 Something that looks spontaneously natural, i.e. you just happen to look up and smile at the camera – with hair that looks natural too, not too well groomed.
3 Simple in clothing terms. Plain colours, not patterns, just a simple plain tee shirt can do it.
4 Nothing like a formal, studio shot. If you are looking at a friend, you should be looking at the camera – but not 'posing' for the camera.
5 Grainy rather than soft focus. Soft focus is too vain; grainy is more flattering if it looks as if the shot has been captured by accident.

TOO UNATTRACTIVE FOR SOCIAL-NETWORKING

According to a March 2010 survey commissioned by weight loss company, LighterLife, one in ten of us decline to use a photo of ourselves as a profile picture, opting instead for an avatar or cartoon drawing or a photo of our dog because of insecurity in how we look. Ten per cent of us also put up out-of-date photos of ourselves so that people think we look younger. Incredibly, five per cent of the 2,000 people questioned even admitted to uploading pictures of a better-looking friend to attract more attention from the opposite sex.

MY STORY: 'SOMEBODY PUT THEIR PHOTO ON MY PROFILE PAGE!'

Will Skyrme, 22, Recent Graduate, Unemployed

'Only the other day something quite weird and sweet happened to me. I was in the Apple Store in Liverpool One, not really in the market for buying a brand new thousand-pound computer, more just to browse, check my emails, and have a quick glance at Facebook. The Apple stores are great for this – you can just slink in, use the computers and waltz off. The shop attendants know the game but because you're one of many they don't try and intimidate you into leaving the shop. Anyway, I did all I needed to do and wandered out, off to Boots to pick up a new toothbrush. Stupidly I'd left my Facebook account logged in. When I checked Facebook again later the next day, I was shocked to find a brand new profile picture on my page showing a couple of grinning strangers. When I'd left my account on, these passing jokers must have snapped themselves with the laptop webcam and changed my profile picture! It was so bizarre and funny that I've left it up for the moment. Perhaps I'll bump into them around Liverpool one day, after all, now I know those big grins a mile off!'

RULE TWO: Adopt a Status Style

Your status style says as much about you as the photo you choose to present to the social-networking world. Are you going to be mysterious or chatty, a regular updater, or sporadic, inspiring or homely? Everyone likes to think their updating style is unique and will entertain, inform or enrich their friends' lives. However, there are certain basic updating mistakes that are guaranteed to get social-networking hackles up. Here is a list of what NOT to do with your status updates:

1. MOUNT A RUNNING COMMENTARY ON YOUR MUNDANE LIFE

'Joe Bloggs just finished breakfast', 'Joe Bloggs is contemplating a mid-morning snack', 'Joe Bloggs is thinking "Only two hours until lunch"'… See the fatal flaw in this line of updating? It's mind-numbingly, paint-dryingly boring. No one wants to know that you popped to Tesco after work, or that you're tweeting while at the checkout. We are just not interested. Geddit? And even more than being boring, it monopolises everyone's news feed to the extent that you'll probably find 99.99 per cent of your 'friends' have in fact opted to 'hide' your updates (and the 0.01 who didn't – well that's your mother, and she's only kept you because you account for 50 per cent of her friends list).

2. Use quotes from famous writers and philosophers

No, no, no, no, noooooooooh! We don't need to know that Eliot thought April was the cruellest month or John-Paul Sartre's take on death, or rather we might need to know that, but not on a social-networking page that also tells you that someone just bought you a Sex on the Beach and your field urgently needs farrowing. Quoting great thinkers doesn't turn you into a great thinker, it turns you into a someone with nothing original to say.

3. Try to create an air of mystery

'Jane Doe thinks it's overrated', 'Jane Doe hopes she makes the right decision', 'Jane Doe is wondering why'. Yes, and Jane Doe should stop thinking she can make her life sound more interesting than it is by being deliberately ambiguous.

4. Big yourself up

'Bob Bighead just got hit on by a top model!', 'Bob Bighead has ordered in the champagne after making the deal of a lifetime', 'Bob Bighead is wondering how to spend his bonus. Weekend in Vegas anyone?' Even if all your boasts are true (and let's face it, not many actually believe you), no one wants to have your achievements and good fortune shoved down their throats every time they log into their Facebook account. When are you going to realise, no one likes a bragger. Far more effective to have understated status updates accompanied by photos that tell their own story (Bob in flash car, Bob with gaggle of gorgeous girls). That way, not only does everyone know what a great life you have, they also think you're endearingly modest about it. Win-win!

5. CARRY OUT PERSONAL VENDETTAS

'Vikki Viper thinks Suzy should repay the £100 she owes', 'Vikki Viper can't understand why her mum is acting so mean', 'Vikki Viper wishes her boss would lighten up'. If your status update is constantly used as a vehicle for lambasting anyone who winds you up, you'll soon find your friends list rapidly depleting. No one wants to hear you complain about other people if there's a good chance that tomorrow or the next day, they themselves might be on the receiving end of your online scorn. Use your status updates for being positive (and save your bitching for your private messages).

6. MAKE SOCIAL PLANS

'Polly Popular says meet up at 7.30, usual place, I'm buying', 'Polly Popular needs a lift to Kelly's party – can't go on public transport dressed as a Vampire Bride!', 'Polly Popular is exhausted after the weekend of excess – who wants to veg out with a pizza and the box set of *Mad Men*?' Yes, it might be a quick way of making sure your social life runs like clockwork, but don't kid yourself that's the motivation behind your status style. Really, what you're saying is 'Look how full my life is! Look how many friends I have! I don't have a second to sit around being bored or lonely!' By making sure everyone knows what a whirlwind your social life is, you're ensuring that many of your 'friends' will feel excluded. Your updates will be like a window onto your marvellous world, against which they're expected to press their noses up and gaze longingly. No one wants their news feed to make them feel inadequate about their own lives, or excluded from someone else's.

DO OTHER PEOPLE'S STATUS UPDATES MAKE US FEEL INADEQUATE? THE EXPERTS SPEAK...

YES SAYS PSYCHOLOGIST DR ARIC SIGMAN

'People are very likely to present an idealised image. There's a lot of one-upmanship going on and it's creating a lot of competitive anxiety and unhappiness. There's an instinct in humans to compare and compete based on what we really know, such as that the people next door have a better sofa.

'But once you get into the virtual world with unnatural "friends" you have a much larger group to compare yourself with so in many ways you are forced to big yourself up, because that's the way the comparison economy goes – otherwise you're left as a little fish in the big pond.

'Though many of these descriptions may be fake, what seems to happen is that young people might feel a sense of failure in not measuring up. If they're still developing their identity and the feedback they are getting is distorted, then this is not going to make them happy or secure. Nor is it good for their self-esteem.'

YES SAYS SOCIAL PSYCHOLOGIST DR ARTHUR CASSIDY

'We always want to create a more positive image of who we are, so there's a bias towards exaggerating certain features of our lives. We all buy into this because we socially compare ourselves every day of our lives to others: "She's got nicer hair", "He's got a great body". Yet clearly this can be destructive, because it makes us feel worse about ourselves.'

MAYBE SAYS DR KAROL SZLICHINSKI, A PSYCHOLOGIST
SPECIALISING IN NEW TECHNOLOGY

'Some people use their status updates to present an idealised image to the world, in the same way they used to send out those circular Christmas letters. But others may well be quite honest about some aspects of their lives. As for it making us feel inferior in some way, while some people will always feel that everyone else is having a better life, most of us are fairly immune to it and don't react that way.

'However, if you're feeling particularly insecure and have stayed home all weekend, and see photos of friends partying and having a good time, it will only add to your feelings of vulnerability.'

STATUS UPDATE

This is like your own personal soap box. You can use it for sounding off about a burning political issue of the day, or commenting on the latest episode of *EastEnders*, or just bemoaning the fact that all your socks are in the wash at the same time. But while it can be a great way of disseminating information or making your views known, or just letting off steam, it pays to recognise that it has its limitations.

ALWAYS REMEMBER

DON'T think that tweeting or Facebooking is the same thing as personal contact. 'There's a problem when people use status updates as a substitute for communication, such as finding out you've been dumped when a partner upgrades their status to "single"', says Dr Karol Szlichinski.

DO be discreet. 'Normally, we are very circumspect about what we give away about ourselves to others, but social-network sites encourage us to disclose information,' says independent addictions counsellor and psychotherapist Dr David Smallwood. 'That isn't necessarily a bad thing – transparency in life is better than hiding things. But if you're fifteen and you've just told the world, via Facebook, that your mother is having breast implants, she's not going to be too pleased!'

RULE THREE: Think before you Upload.

Been to a kicking party? Just come back from two weeks in Ibiza? Seen your sister get married, or your nephew turn twenty-one? What's the first thing you're going to want to do the second you get home? Upload your photos onto your social-networking profile page. And what's the second thing you're going to want to do? Delete all the ones in which you a) have bad hair, b) have multiple chins or c) are making one of those self-conscious faces we all pull when we see a camera lens pointed in our direction. According to the March 2010 LighterLife survey, nearly half of us remove pictures which don't show us in the very best light. Fourteen per cent of women also admit to de-tagging photos so they don't show up on their profile page, while one in ten claimed to feel 'sick' when looking at photos of themselves online.

The paradox of photo-culling, though, is that while we're ruthless when it comes to pictures that show us in a less-than-flattering light, we fail to apply the same judicious editing to other areas. For example, we rarely stop to consider whether it's entirely wise to post photos of last night's marathon drinking session when we've just cried off from meeting Mum for lunch, claiming overwork (whose ridiculous idea was it anyway to 'friend' a parent? Of which more later). Most of us operate a very lax vetting procedure when it comes to uploading photos. Basically, if there's a choice between publishing and be damned, and going through every one of those 1,000-plus photos one by one, which are you going to choose?

That's why, for many of us, the photo gallery on our social-networking page becomes the equivalent of a photo-diary, recording in pictures the progress of our daily (and nightly lives). And what could possibly be wrong with that?

Well, quite a lot of things actually. Such as:

- Inevitably, some people are going to feel left out. Even if the photos just show you and your mate lying on the sofa the morning after the night before, wearing big fluffy slippers and pained expressions, somebody somewhere is going to be thinking, 'A sleepover? Why wasn't I invited?'

- Once a photo goes up, it's in the public domain. Even if, after a few hours of sober reflection, you decide it's not such a good idea to share that hilarious photo of you balancing on a traffic bollard in the middle of the A1 wearing a paper crown and pretending to be the Statue of Liberty, and delete it from your gallery, it's too late to stop other people from seeing it, and even passing it on. Your friends will think it amusing. Your boss, on the other hand, might have other ideas.

- While you may have given your photos a clean bill of health after a cursory once-over to make sure you're not doing anything untoward, you may not have given all the people in the pictures similar consideration. Should your married colleague really have been giving the new intern such an intensive debriefing in those after-work pub photos? Will your sister appreciate that shot of her wearing the necklace she then wrapped up and gave to your mum as a birthday gift?

RULE FOUR: Don't Overdo It

FarmVille, quizzes, honesty boxes, poking, superpoking, buying drinks/pets/Christmas trees... While your friends will doubtless be thrilled to know they're in your thoughts, do they really need to know you've sent them a flowery heart, or watered their crops, or slung some dog poo at them, or nominated them as Person Most Likely To Wear Out a Pair of FlipFlops?

As with many things in life, when it comes to social-networking, less is often more. Unless you're under the age of 12, deluging your nearest and dearest with unwanted virtual gifts and invitations to applications they would have uploaded themselves if they'd been the teensiest bit interested is not going to make them feel special. It's more likely to make them feel highly irritated. Oh, and it might also give them the impression that you have very little else of importance in your rather sad, empty life.

If your friends log onto their Facebook page in the evening to find the results of 25 different quizzes you've taken that day, from which *Friends* character you most resemble to what your native American Indian name might be, they're not going to think 'Wow, I'd never have guessed XX would be that kind of serial killer'; they're going to think, 'I wish XX would get a life and stop clogging up my news feed'. See the difference?

Similarly, if they wake up on their birthday to a list of birthday greetings from various friends, they're probably going to be chuffed. But if they wake up to a list of birthday greetings plus virtual hugs, virtual champagne cocktails, a whole host of presents to unwrap, a cuddly teddy holding a message, a snow globe, fairy wishes and the news that you've nominated them to receive daily inspirational quotes direct to their home page, they're going to feel just a little bit overwhelmed.

When it comes to social-networking extras, it definitely pays to go for quality rather than quantity.

THE HIDDEN MEANING OF EMOTICONS

Those little faces you can add to your text on social-networking sites to emphasise your meaning in the absence of physical gestures and body language, may sound like a great idea, but as with all the other gimmicks, overuse can sometimes lead to trouble. According to body language and behavioural expert Judi James, there's a hidden message behind every emoticon. And it can say quite a lot about the person using it…

- SMILE: You use this because you want to appear positive, upbeat and optimistic. But remember, this symbol is often used by people who are either apologising for a criticism or those who are lacking in genuine humour. If you have to show people you're being funny, your communications skills might need a re-boot!
- FROWN: You think you're saying you're stressed or under pressure. But are you so full of disapproval of so many things you're using this to illustrate it?
- GASP: How often, in real life, do we really gasp? Why are you pretending it's common for you? Using this is infantile and ditzy. You're trying to 'up' the drama of the most everyday situations by appearing to be shocked.
- GRIN: Ah, the cool, knowing, rather sexy dude. At least, that's

17

how the user likes to see themselves. Using this indicates you're sharing the joke – but in a slightly sly way, suggesting a gossip. Or a rumour-monger.

- SUNGLASSES: In a word, why? You probably don't know why, meaning you're both confused and a tad pretentious. Unless there's bright light around, we wear shades to look remote and/or famous. With this emoticon, you are the internet version of Bono.

- PENGUIN: Top of the 'Well it seems like a good idea but I can't tell you why' list, a blend of remote, cute, untouchable, funny, even glacial. In other words, you're so hard to get to know, you don't even know yourself very well!

- CONFUSED: You really do want to come across as cute, in a Hugh Grant kind of way. People using this, however, are only playing at being confused. In reality, they're sharp as a tack. But very strategic.

- SHARK: Predatory, competitive. Someone who tries, year in, year out, to get onto *The Apprentice*.

- PACMAN: A traditionalist with retrospective tastes and values. Hoping to be seen as ironic and cool.

- ROBOT: No logical, intellectual thinker would use this. This is someone pretending to be clever.

- WINK: A gesture of collusion, aimed at doing some subliminal bonding, by getting the other person in on the joke.

- KISS: A cross signoff turns into a kiss. A non-sexual kiss, though – more like a kiss for your annoying, embarrassing auntie.

- GRUMPY: Take this at face value, it's not ironic. This person is mean, miserable, moody and grumpy, but hoping others will somehow find their curmudgeonliness appealing, just because they've 'fessed up' to it.

- ANGEL/DEVIL: Like a bluff in poker. Whichever one is used, you can assume the opposite.
- CRY: Whatever happened to the British stiff upper lip? At least it's a warning what the main thrust of communication is going to be, i.e. 'me, me, poor me, etc.' A good candidate for Piers Morgan.
- HEART: Advertising your nurturing qualities to the world is deeply suspicious. If you're genuinely in love and sending these you're not cute, just soppy.

Twitterquette

Twitter prides itself on being different from Facebook and other social-networking sites, so the complicated rules of Twitterdom deserve singling out. Many Twitter virgins sign up to the site but take one look at it and run screaming (or virtually screaming) back to the familiarity of Facebook, but actually Twitter is very straightforward once you've mastered the basic rules.

10 BASIC RULES OF TWITTER

1 People who are interested in you and sign up to read your tweets are called 'followers'.
2 If you are interested in someone, you can 'follow' them.
3 You have 140 characters or less to record your thoughts or actions.
4 You can either 'tweet' people you know, or find people who interest you to follow and tweet.
5 You reply to tweets using the @ symbol followed by the username.
6 You share other people's tweets using RT followed by the @ symbol and their user name.
7 You can tweet via mobile using SMS or your Wi-Fi.

8 You can send private messages to your followers.

9 Shy Twitterers can protect their updates so that only approved followers can read them.

10 Typing a hash key before a word or phrase will create a link taking followers to other recent tweets on that subject.

HOW TO JOIN THE TWITTERATI

- Choose wisely when it comes to the profile pic. Basically the photo on your Twitter page is very small so KEEP IT SIMPLE. Head shot = good. Group shot of you and your friends in front of the Taj Mahal = rubbish.

- Twitter gives you the additional option of choosing a background design for your page. You can either go for one of the generic options supplied by Twitter, or upload an image of your own. Again it pays to keep it simple and stylish. Let your words do the talking, not your background images.

- The great thing about the Twitter biography is you have a maximum limit of 140 characters, so you can't waffle on about how you got your cycling proficiency or go into detail about your philosophy on life, the universe and everything.

TWITTER DO'S AND DON'TS

- **DO** tweet regularly but pithily – leave it too long between tweets and your followers will give up and go away. Then again, treat them to a minute-by-minute account of your progression through the roadworks on the M25 and they might decide to follow someone more exciting instead, like @watchpaintdry.

- **DON'T** tweet yourself up. Modestly mentioning a special achievement is one thing, but tweeting your own trumpet constantly, even if it's just bragging about how many Twitter followers you have, is not going to endear you to anyone.

- **DO** tweet rather than just lurk – it's meant to be an interactive site, not a voyeuristic one.
- **DON'T** tweet mundane comments about meet-up times and arrangements, save the personal stuff for private messages otherwise the majority of your followers are going to start to feel excluded.
- **DO** stop confusing 'following' with 'stalking'. It's okay to follow celebrities you don't know. If they didn't want that, they wouldn't be on Twitter in the first place.

MY STORY: 'A STRANGER PICKED A FIGHT WITH ME ON TWITTER!'

Katy Parry, 23, PA

'I never thought it would happen to me, but I'm finally starting to see the point of Twitter. For years I've been trying to get myself into the world of blogging and twitter and flickr and all those things but there's been a little something holding me back – perhaps it just feels all too contrived, or at least it did. Recently though, I've been starting to get quite into Twitter and following loads of people. But the weird thing is that you often get the most random people following you. I once tweeted something about *The X Factor*, nothing controversial, but this random follower from Norwich got completely outraged and started tweeting angrily at me left, right and centre. I couldn't understand what I'd done to provoke her but when I went on her page I realised she'd done it to loads of people, in fact she seemed to make a hobby of starting fights with complete strangers! Bizarre!'

MY STORY: 'MY TWITTER PEST TURNED OUT TO BE MY EX-TEACHER!'

Emily Doyle, 24, Shop Assistant

'I started a Twitter account, not in my own name but as a place to post music reviews. I go to a lot of gigs and review things on the side occasionally so I figured why not have a running Twitter account that I can tweet my musical musings on? It did quite well, got listed by a couple of people and now it's got a good few followers. Anyway, I guess it's just the nature of Twitter but quite a lot of my followers often regularly tweet back to me with their thoughts on what I've said. There is one follower in particular that really annoys me. Now I know I shouldn't say that but this particular guy just seems to have the worst taste. He's always suggesting rubbish tracks for me to listen to, and never quite gets it when I say something, always semi-misinterpreting my point. Anyway, I tweeted I was going to this gig and much to my dismay he retweeted it seconds later and said he was going as well. I knew it could be a possibility that he knew what I looked like because I'd put photos up occasionally if they happened to fit in or be really good, but I wasn't going to let this ruin a gig I was really looking forward to. The night rolled around and the gig was great and I'd completely forgotten about this guy until as I was leaving someone grabbed my arm. I turned around and froze. 'Hi,' he said, 'are you the music savvy who I follow on Twitter?' I just stood there dumbfounded. It was my Year Four teacher from primary school! Amazingly, he didn't recognise me, he just knew me as the music blogger on Twitter. Excruciatingly embarrassed I denied it was me, and legged it. The worst thing was that he'd been one of my favourite teachers!'

'O Romeo, Romeo, wherefore art thou ?... Not on Facebook !'

2

Love – When It All Goes Right

L ove is a many-splendoured thing. Especially when it's shared with seven or eight hundred of your very closest online friends.

If there had been Facebook when Romeo was wooing Juliet, how different would things have been? No need for Juliet to shiver on a balcony when she could be tucked up on her sofa in one of those blankets-with-sleeves chatting with her beau on her laptop.

Juliet Capulet: Romeo where4 art u?

Romeo Montague: Hanging wiv da Montague bruvvas. Wassup babes? *(sent by Facebook mobile)*

And if Cleopatra had been able to tweet to Anthony that she wasn't dead after all (@queencleopatra: OMG, still alive!), if he could have followed the link to her updated-every-minute blog http://cleo4eva.com) would he have been so quick to fall on his sword?

Love in the time of social-networking is a complicated affair.

On the one hand, Bebo, Facebook, MySpace etc. have broadened our romantic horizons to the extent that it's possible to hook up with Mr Right on the other side of the world with one click of a mouse, just because he happens to be your friend's brother's boss's cousin (*Wow! Such a coincidence. It's fate!*). But the downside is that when Mr Right turns out to be Mr Very, Very Wrong and proves it by posting photos of you on his profile page, passed out after the Christmas party and wearing little more than a paper hat and a slack expression, it's a horribly public kind of humiliation.

Finding Love

It's hard to believe that just a generation ago, looking for love entailed actually (gasp) leaving the house. Now thanks to the wonders of social-networking, we no longer need to go searching; instead it arrives fully uploaded and tagged directly into our news feed. A survey conducted in July 2010 by Light Speed Research for Oxygen Media found that 65 per cent of men and 50 per cent of women use Facebook to find romance.

A separate 2009 survey of 3,000 people aged between 20 and 40, conducted by internet market research company www.OnePoll.com, revealed some further surprising statistics about romance in the era of social-networking:

- 75 per cent of us believe there are fewer stigmas attached to meeting a love-match via Facebook, Friends Reunited or Bebo than normal internet-dating websites like match.com.
- One in four were dating – or had dated – someone they met through online community websites and over a third had got back in touch with an old flame through the sites.

- 10 per cent had embarked on an affair or a one-night stand with someone they met via a social-networking site.
- 46 per cent believed it was easier to meet someone through social-networking sites than in the flesh. Of these, 57 per cent admitted they were more confident communicating with a potential suitor online, with more than a third saying it enabled them to get to know someone before meeting them.
- 27 per cent felt using social-networking sites cut down the time to find love compared to having to having to meet prospective partners face to face, with 44 per cent pronouncing it 'cooler' to do it that way.
- A quarter confessed to purposely uploading flattering pictures of themselves in the hope of a potential love interest spotting their profile.

Anyone looking to attract a suitor via social-networking will find themselves investing an awful lot of time and effort into picking a picture that not only makes them look drop-dead gorgeous, but also sends out the kind of image they imagine will attract their ideal mate. So, if your idea of Mr/Ms Perfect is sporty, you might put up that photo of you crossing the 10K finishing line (*just Photoshop out those unsightly sweat patches*). For those looking to attract a more arty, creative type, you might decide on a photo of your latest still-life or the cover of your band's newest CD.

But nothing is more of a handy guide for would-be suitors than the photo gallery. At a glance, you can find out what kind of friends your potential beloved has, where they socialise, what their family looks like and which of their clothes are definitely destined for the bin should you ever get together.

The trouble with finding love through a networking website is that what you see isn't always what you get, says psychologist, Dr Aric Sigman.

'The difference is that when you see someone in the normal way, you immediately know their voice, their looks, their smile, all the things that are essential to attraction – or being repelled – by someone,' he says.

'On networking sites people put their best face on when advertising their sexual wares. So when they want to offer themselves up for relationships, they are very unlikely to offer up photos that are highly unflattering or describe themselves in unattractive terms.

'What social-networking has done is to encourage people to present themselves in a polished way and to objectify themselves. So you've "airbrushed" your image. And this can be an obstacle to forming relationships because ultimately you still have to meet the person and see what they really look or sound like. Often, the two things have nothing in common.'

Dr Sigman believes that in some cases, social-networking does fulfil a necessary romantic function.

'As was the case with lonely-hearts columns and penpals, there are a significant number of people who don't take well to meeting people face to face the first time around. Society will always have a number of people who are not party animals, shy people. For those people social-networking can be a useful first step in filtering the selection of possible candidates down to a manageable number without having to go through the agonising process of meeting face to face.'

However, he warns that sooner or later, a face-to-face meeting is essential before deciding whether or not Cupid has struck gold:

'Human chemistry is something that is very hard to transmit through the electronic media. There's a "magic" that attracts people and it's very hard to get that in other ways than meeting face to face. Even speed dating, scientifically, has more going for it than social-networking; people can get a sense of whether there's any basic chemistry there. You just can't get that through social-networking.'

Some people argue that social-networking, in a purely practical sense, is a wonderful romantic aid. 'There's nothing "new" about social-networking, we've done it since we were born, networking just means extending your friendship base,' says social psychologist, Dr Arthur Cassidy. 'But the computer now facilitates so many more opportunities for us. It's a much more novel sense of finding new friends in different places – people you might not find in your own home town.'

However, he too warns that social-networking might be interfering in our tried-and-tested strategies for meeting a mate. 'In the days before social-networking we had to use our normal skills of attraction, meeting someone, you might like their personality, their smile, their humour – that's how we'd normally fall in love. We depended on natural sexual attraction.'

THE FIVE TYPES MOST LIKELY TO BE LOOKING FOR LOVE ON A SOCIAL-NETWORKING SITE:

1 **The Bottom Feeder (no, that doesn't mean what you think it does).** He might already have one relationship on the go. He might even have several, but he can't resist cruising along in the depths of the social-networking scene, imbibing whatever other romantic titbits might cross his path.

2 **The True Romantic.** Somewhere, somehow there is the perfect someone for her, and somehow, some way, she will find him. She scours groups pages, looking for anyone who shares her interests, cross referencing the lists of fans against other groups she also belongs to. She analyses photos, updates, quiz results, on the alert for the giveaway signs that will show her that this is The One.

3 **The Lazy Lover.** He quite wants a relationship, and would quite like not to be in on another Saturday night watching *Strictly Come Dancing* in his tracky bottoms, but when it comes to actually getting dressed up and going out in search of company… well, he just can't really be bothered. That's where this social-networking thing comes in handy – all those potential girlfriends just waiting to hear from him, *and he doesn't even have to get off the sofa!* What a result!

4 **The Love Ladder Climber**. She just *loves* the way social-networking sites show her exactly how to trade up in the love stakes – and who to trade up to. At a glance she can spot a potential new boyfriend's social scene, what he does for a living, the kind of car he drives, the places he goes on holiday. And if that compares favourably to her current beau, well she can change that just as fast as you can say 'XX is Single'.

5 **The Cheapskate Charmer.** It's all very well having a girlfriend and being in a relationship, but blimey it's expensive. All that wining and dining and sending flowers and buying presents. Which is where social-networking is so wonderful – you can make all those romantic gestures *without spending a penny*! Send her a virtual cocktail, a beautiful bouquet of roses, a sweet, cuddly teddy attached to a sentimental rosette. Be as indulgent

and as extravagant as you like, and it still won't make a dent in your bank balance. It's win/win all the way – she gets to be treated like a princess, and your wallet gets to stay firmly wedged in your back pocket. And who said romance was dead?

SOCIAL-NETWORKING FOR COMMITMENT-PHOBES: AN EXPERT SPEAKS

Dr Karol Szlichinski is a psychologist specialising in new technology, who believes that though social-networking has become increasingly part of our 'repertoire' of finding love, it raises serious commitment issues.

'The connections via social-networking with people one doesn't know are very easy to make – and until people actually meet face to face there's no kind of personal bond, which makes it easy to break those connections. Basically there's very little commitment until people do meet. It can happen remotely, but the messaging capabilities of sites like Twitter are quite limited, so people often shift to electronic mail to learn more.

'But if people are just exchanging very short messages via a social-networking site, those do not give very much space to reveal much; there's not much invested in that kind of messaging. So you wouldn't expect a lot of commitment to underlie it.

'If you meet someone through work or friends, you have a shared social context, other people who know both of you and may take a view if things go badly. Just meeting someone off the net, someone could be treated very badly – and no one would know.'

| MY STORY: 'HE LIED TO GET ME TO GO OUT WITH HIM' |

Rosie Gizauakas, 23, Journalist

'I used to work for my university in their call centre, calling up previous students and fundraising for the university. It was well paid, only a few hours a week and I was working with some of my friends too so I didn't really mind it. I called up one old student who I had to talk to for ages. I wasn't convinced he was going to give any money, but as he kept talking I couldn't really hang up on him, so I sort of humoured him as he chatted away. He began to get a bit flirty but I didn't rise to it and eventually got him off the phone. Anyway, just as part of routine (even though he didn't donate any money) we send an email saying, 'Thank you for talking to us etc. etc. etc.' to everybody we've spoken to that day. A few days later I had a Facebook add from a boy whose name sounded sort of familiar, and it came with a message saying we'd met at a party and he'd love to go out for a drink. It didn't take me long to clock it was Mr Talkative from work, I can't believe he thought he could actually lie and I wouldn't notice!'

A MATCH MADE ON LOVEBOOK

Star-crossed lovers all over the world have reasons to thank the social-networking sites that played cupid to their romance. Couples who double-clicked their way to love include:

1. KELLY HILDEBRANDT AND, ER... KELLY HILDEBRAND

Feeling at a loose end one evening in 2008, 20-year-old Kelly Hildebrand, a female student from Florida, decided to type her name into the search bar on Facebook, to see if anyone else shared the same name. Kelly Hildebrandt, a 24-year-old male financial services worker from Texas, was a near-perfect match so she decided on a whim to send him a message: 'Hi. We have the same name. Thought it was cool.'

Intrigued by the message and by the 'cute' profile picture that accompanied it, He Kelly responded and soon the couple were exchanging emails as if they'd known each other forever. The emails led to phone calls, the calls led to visits and, in December, a few months after She Kelly sent her first email, she found a diamond engagement ring hidden in a treasure box on a beach.

2. NEIL HARWOOD AND LIZ GAVIN

When Neil Harwood, 36, spotted a photo of beauty therapist Liz Gavin, 31, on Facebook, he was immediately smitten and cheekily sent her a friend request. Liz assumed she knew him and added him before checking out his page and realising she didn't have a clue who he was. Moments later, Neil, who is in the Royal Navy, sent her a message, and the couple began cyber-talking. Three months later, they were engaged.

And if you thought social-networking sites were just for the commoners, celebrities are also finding love online:

1. KERRY KATONA

After a bitter and very public split from Mark Croft, former Atomic Kitten star and mum-of-four Kerry apparently got together with Adam Waldron, a painter and decorator, through the wonders of Facebook.

2. GREGG WALLACE

Masterchef presenter Gregg Wallace found love with one of his 2,000 Twitter followers after posting a message about 'jiggling cabbage' on his Twitter page. Biology teacher Heidi Brown sent him a message, to which he replied, 'Jiggling cabbage is not a euphemism. No more than shuffling shallots or sorting celery.' Before long the two tweeters had arranged to meet and Brown moved in with Wallace, who uses the Twitter name PuddingFace, after just a few months.

However, not all stars are so enamoured of the role social-networking plays in modern romance. Hollywood star Drew Barrymore, for example, reckons sites like MySpace and Facebook take the mystery out of falling in love. 'I just don't like this compulsive, instantaneous, over-information, lack-of-privacy, weirdo aspect of the world,' she told *Marie Claire* magazine in September 2010. 'If you meet someone, they already know everything. What about showing up on the date and saying, "What do you do for a living? Who are your friends?" Yes, you can avoid maybe a serial killer but who f***ing knows?'

SOCIAL-NETWORKING GOLDEN LOVE RULE: DON'T PRETEND TO BE SOMEONE YOU'RE NOT

When it comes to looking for love, everyone wants to present themselves in the best possible light, which is fine – just as long as you don't present yourself as someone else altogether. The internet is full of disgruntled would-be lovers who fell in love with someone they met on a social-networking site, only to discover that the photo they've been swooning over through the long nights of frantic email exchange actually bears no resemblance to the real thing.

FAKE PHOTO CASE ONE:

'I recently met a fantastic man on MySpace but made the stupid mistake of using someone else's pic as I'm insecure about how I look. We chatted on the phone for four months and he's just found out about me lying over the pictures. He said he'd fallen in love with my personality and didn't care how I looked, but now he wants nothing more to do with me.'

FAKE PHOTO CASE TWO:

'Turns out a woman I was talking to on Facebook for months had sent me her beautiful sister's picture. I know looks aren't important, but that picture was what I was initially attracted to. Now I'm due to meet this woman, but I don't know what to do as her sister lives across the street.'

FINDING LOVE ON A SOCIAL-NETWORKING SITE: AN EXPERT'S WARNING:

Dr David Smallwood, independent addiction counsellor and psychotherapist, warns that people who seek out love via social-networking run the risk of being totally misled:

'How can you possibly know if someone loves you down a broadband connection? On Facebook you can be anyone you want. Cyrano de Bergerac thought he was a monster so he used someone else to woo the woman he loved. He had the words – but that was all. In a similar way, someone on Facebook can write all the right words, but you don't have the same opportunity as when you meet someone in person to see whether the words that are spoken match the body language. A man can be ever so brave telling an 18-stone wrestler that he's a complete twat on Facebook. But if he met him on the street, he'd be legging it in the opposite direction! It's the same principle when you're talking about romance.'

IN A RELATIONSHIP

There was a time when couples could work out over a series of dates how their relationship was progressing, but in the new era of social-networking, entering into a relationship is a much simpler affair. You simply click the box for 'in a relationship with X', a message gets sent to X to confirm and, hey presto, the whole world (including X) knows the two of you are now an item.

'I went out for a drink with a bloke a couple of weeks ago,' says 24-year-old Sammie Knight from Warrington. 'We had a snog, but nothing more. Then that night I had a Facebook request from him asking for us to be listed as "in a relationship". I thought, "Hang on a minute. All we had was a snog and a couple of glasses of wine. That doesn't equal a relationship, and I certainly don't want my parents, work colleagues and all my mates thinking I'm involved with someone they've never even heard of before."'

Nevertheless, so ingrained has this practice become, that there are growing numbers of people who don't actually believe a relationship exists unless it is confirmed by Facebook. Witness the Facebook Groups with names such as: 'If Your Relationship Isn't Listed in

Facebook it doesn't Count', or 'A Relationship Isn't Official Unless It's Facebook Verified' or the pithy 'Your Relationship: It's Not Official Until Facebook News feed Says So'.

But 'in a relationship' isn't the only option available when it comes to declaiming love status. You can also choose from Single, Married, Engaged, It's Complicated, In an Open Relationship, Widowed, Separated or Divorced.

However, that's not enough for some people. The Facebook Groups list abounds with people up in arms about how restrictive the list is and bursting with suggestions of new options to add.

OPTIONS PEOPLE WANT TO SEE ADDED TO THE RELATIONSHIP STATUS LIST:

Desperate
Player
Waiting for Mr Right
In a Romance with
Is Flirting With
Done With
Being Led On By
Is Waiting
In Love With
Soul mates
Has No Idea What's Going On
Heartbroken
Has a Crush On
Under The Thumb Of
Having an Affair With
Is Two Timing With

I Wish I Knew
Rebounding
Friends With Benefits With
More Than Friends But Less Than Lovers
Would Rather Be With
In Negotiations With
Polyamorous
Celibate

Psychologist Dr Aric Sigman believes there's a danger that social-networking can affect the way we deal with our real-life relationships.

'It certainly changes people's expectations for relationships. Being able to click and change the window or defriend has understandably led people to believe subconsciously that if they don't like the way things are going, they can just click something and hey presto – someone will behave differently. It has changed people's expectations of how others conform to their desires and needs.

'Real life is not like that. Real personal relationships are more shades of grey; sometimes you do have to tolerate people not conforming to what you want here and now.

'People who spend too much time running their relationships virtually may find it more difficult to manage them non-virtually, particularly if you're younger and haven't learned how to deal with the real thing. Social-networking is a tool to embellish your social life. But the concern is when it's the social life first time around, without the normal skills you learn in the real world to deal with it.'

MY STORY: 'HIS ROMANTIC FACEBOOK GESTURE RUINED OUR RELATIONSHIP'

Jenni Herzberg, 23, Drama MA Student

I once stopped seeing somebody because of Facebook. It sounds really terrible. Having had a lovely first date with a guy I was anxious to hear from him about our next rendezvous. To my disappointment I found out via a notification on Facebook. His bright idea was to create an event entitled 'Rob and Jenni's second date' – he had made it totally private and I was the only name on the guestlist. What I gather was meant to be taken as a romantic and witty gesture for the modern age was in reality well... just a little creepy. Needless to say I clicked un-attending and never saw him again!

'Tweetheart, Will You Marry Me?

Popping the question is one of the defining moments in any long-term relationship. Nervous lovers have always sweated over setting, timing and, the big one, how to cope with the humiliation of getting a 'no'.

Social-networking sites take away all that angst. You can propose to your beloved without risk of seeing shock, fear or loathing written on their face, and if they say 'no', you can always claim you meant it as a joke (albeit one now shared by hundreds of friends, vague acquaintances and stalkers).

Even better, the rejection, if it comes, carries less sting by virtue of being electronically sent and often restricted to 140 characters.

When American reality TV star Snooki's boyfriend of two weeks proposed by posing topless on the cover of a magazine, with the strapline 'Will you Marry Me?' emblazoned across his bended knee, she responded via her Twitter page – and it wasn't good news for the lovesick Romeo. 'Just want to set the record straight. I'm single and I'm not going to get married.' That would be a 'no' then...

Rachel Status Update

Thanks! It happened before prom, like during the day on satureday. How he asked was really sweet he got some daisys an put them in the ground in the park by my house, so when we went over there to play catch he threw the ball and it landed by the daisys and they spelt out will you marry me. When I turned around he was on his knee with the ring and I ran over to him and gave him a big hug saying yes of course.

Margo

I am so happy for you but you can't spell very well

THE SOCIAL-NETWORKING PROPOSAL – WHAT'S THE POINT?

1 It reduces the risk of humiliating yourself in front of your beloved if she says no. Of course, there's the small drawback of humiliating yourself in front of a few hundred of your online followers but, hey, what's a little embarrassment between Facebook friends?

2 It turns a private proposal into a public performance, allowing each partner access to the advice and suggestions of their online entourage.

3 It's the quickest way of spreading the word to as many people as possible (although you have to be pretty confident of a 'yes' to risk this one).

4 Anyone unsure of getting the answer they're after might be
  hoping that posting a proposal on a public site will strengthen
  their cause by putting their beloved on the spot. Harder to say
  'no' when hundreds of your friends are saying 'Aaaaaaaah!' and
  already shopping for wedding hats.

5 By making a proposal public property, you can always claim
  later that it was all a joke if a) you don't get the response you
  want or b) you sober up.

Facebook Weddings

After the proposal comes the wedding, and social-networking sites
are fast becoming as much a part of modern wedding etiquette as
confetti and prenuptial agreements.

In November 2009, Dana Hanna, a bridegroom from Maryland,
USA, became an internet sensation when he paused midway
through his wedding to update his Twitter and Facebook statuses
from the altar. The YouTube video of the wedding showed the
groom reaching into his pocket for the phone as the minister was
about to pronounce the couple man and wife. 'Oh, Dana is updating
his relationship status on Facebook,' the minister joked, before
continuing: 'As I was saying, I now pronounce you husband and
wife. It's now official on Facebook. It's official in my book. Dana you
may kiss your bride.' Dana's first tweet as a married man read:
'Standing at the altar with @TracyPage where just a second ago, she
became my wife! Gotta go, time to kiss my bride. #weddingday 1:48
PM Nov 21st from Twittelator.'

> **Status Update**
>
> **XXX**
>
> is amused by how many people have messaged her thinking they are coming to the wedding. At $200 per person, you need to speak to me more than once a year 2 come.

Another groom who has a lot to thank social-networking for is Kyle Dias who, according to the *Sun*, managed to organise his entire wedding from his prison cell using a mobile equipped with wireless connection – despite mobile phones being banned from HMP Rochester in Kent, where Dias was serving four months for robbery.

But not everyone is so delighted with social-networking sites' ever-expanding role in wedding culture.

June 2010 saw a thread on popular internet chatroom Mumsnet in which women complained about unflattering wedding photos of them being posted up on Facebook. Some posters even said they'd think twice about attending weddings if there was a risk of photos of double chins and ill-advised dance moves being uploaded onto the internet the following Monday morning.

Guests aren't the only ones to have fallen foul of the new social media wedding rules. More than one bride has found themselves red-faced after disgruntled friends and family have discovered, via Facebook or MySpace, that they've been left off the guest-list.

'Don't you just long for a case of good old
sexual transgression rather than inappropriate
blogs, tweets and chats ?'

3
Love – When It All Goes Wrong

BickerBook

While social-networking sites are fast becoming the modern couple's favourite method of informing the world that love is in the air, the flipside is that they are also the quickest, easiest way of letting off steam when the path of true love isn't running quite so smoothly.

Most of us know at least one couple who lurch from being 'in a relationship' to 'single' with such frequency it's hard to keep track. No sooner have you posted a message commiserating on the latest acrimonious break-up, and agreeing that yes, he is a total b*****d, than there appears a loved-up post announcing the joyful return to loved-up status.

Even celebrity couples (or ex-couples) aren't averse to washing their dirty linen in public (as long as it's less than 140 characters long).

When Lindsay Lohan split up from girlfriend Sam Ronson, she used Twitter to accuse her ex of being unfaithful, apparently posting while the two were staying separately at the exclusive Chateau Marmont Hotel in Los Angeles: 'I was right all along. Cheat.'

This was followed by Li-Lo justifying her twitter rant as being payback for Ronson supposedly talking to the *People* magazine: 'Being cheated on does wonders to you. I'm doing this publicly because u & ur friends call *People*. So you win, you broke my heart. Now go away. I loved you.'

TOP TEN SOCIAL-NETWORKING BICKERS:

1 What do you mean by changing your relationship status? What are you trying to tell me?
2 Who is the girl in that photo? And wasn't that picture taken the night you told me you had to stay home to work?
3 Why did you have to publicise the fact that you just beat me at Scrabble? Are you trying to humiliate me?
4 You never offer to harvest *my* crops...
5 Why did your mum 'like' the update you made about me looking like a complete t**t at that fancy dress party?
6 No, poking him does not mean I want to sleep with him.
7 If you're going to change your profile pic without telling me, can you at least make it one where you're wearing some clothes?
8 Since when have you read *War and Peace*, *Wolf Hall* and *The Complete Works of Shakespeare*?
9 Ha – I'm going to tell everyone that your favourite film is NOT *Citizen Kane*, it's *Dude Where's My Car*.
10 I told you about my koumpounophobia in confidence – not so that you could update your status with 'OMG, my boyfriend's afraid of BUTTONS!'

Jesse is single

Eric

We done? You dumping me like this?

Betrayal

With more and more of us finding the loves of our lives on social-networking sites, it follows that more and more of us are also using the same sites to find people with whom to cheat on the loves of our lives.

Putting it simply, social-networking has been a gift for adulterers.

But social-networking is a double-edged sword for love cheats, for while it's easier to find extra-curricular partners, it's also much easier to get caught.

In Atlanta, USA, two teachers were forced to take 'administrative leave' after getting into a physical brawl over a love letter posted on the Facebook page of the man both claimed to be romantically involved with.

Teacher Chaka Cobb, who claimed to be expecting a child with the man, a fellow teacher at the school where both women taught, was outraged when she found a letter from Ebony Smith on her lover's Facebook page. 'I am in love with you. I am tired of being your every blue moon ****' was what the letter said. In response, Cobb posted an angry message which made no secret of what she thought of her rival.

Not surprisingly, the atmosphere was strained when the two women met in the school hall the following Monday morning and a fight broke out, leading to both women facing police charges.

A recent survey by travel firm travelsupermarket.com revealed that one in ten people under 20 years old had cheated on partners abroad, and one in five of those had later been tracked down and outed on networking sites like Facebook. Half of the holidaymakers questioned admitted they didn't give out personal details while away for fear of being stalked online by their holiday romance.

Break-up

If there's one thing worse than learning that you're in a relationship via Facebook, it is logging on to find you're unexpectedly single. A 2009 poll by loveheart.com found that 50 per cent of under 21s and nearly one in five aged 22–30 had publicly dumped their other halves through Facebook or Twitter. Another survey conducted by dating application AreYouInterested (comprising 1,000 respondents, of which 70 per cent were men) found that:

- Almost 25 per cent of respondents found out their own relationship was over by seeing it on Facebook first.
- Around 21 per cent of respondents said they would carry out a Facebook break-up by changing their status to single.
- Nearly 40 per cent of respondents had updated their status on Facebook so the person they're dating saw they had plans.
- And almost 35 per cent of respondents had used their Facebook status to make someone think they had plans, even if they didn't.

At the same time, according to the July 2010 survey conducted by Light Speed Research for Oxygen Media, 24 per cent of men break up through Facebook as opposed to 9 per cent of the women.

Status Update

Nick is no longer listed as 'in a relationship'

Anne Marie

ohh... when the f**k did we break up? Whatever!

Nick

When I see you Monday

Break-up etiquette on social-networking sites often involves a bitter power struggle over who dumps who first. Many's the conniving partner who changes their relationship status to 'single' *before* informing their former partner of the fact, to be sure of getting updated first.

Status Update

Matt

Love isn't easy. NOT a good day. I need a drink

(✓Geri likes this)

Geri

Ruining another relationship? Did NOT see that coming

Kristen

Your just jealous he chose me over ur fugly ass

Geri

A 26 year old with no job and a stupid goatee. I don't know how ill live without him!

Matt

My goatee isn't stupid

A TYPICAL FACEBOOK BREAK-UP GOES SOMETHING LIKE THIS:

1 Change relationship status to 'single'.

2 Post message actually breaking up with partner.

3 Change profile pic from cute pic of the two of you together, to sexy pic of you pouting into camera.

4 Defriend ex-partner.

5 Message all your friends to make sure they defriend him too.

6 De-tag yourself from all photos that include your ex (don't want to deter new suitors).

7 List yourself as 'in a relationship' with one of your best friends of the opposite sex (it helps to get their permission first), so that a) your ex sees how quickly you've moved on and b) you don't have to see the word 'single' on your page every time you log on. Don't worry about seeming sad, fake relationships are on the increase on social-networking sites.

MY STORY: 'MY FRIEND INVENTED A GIRLFRIEND TO WIN BACK HIS EX'

Mohammed Chhoangali, 21, medical trainee

'I had a friend when we were younger that tried to piss off his ex-girlfriend by creating a new one on MySpace. Yes – that is literally how sad we all were when we were 14. Now you have to understand a few things, when I say "ex-girlfriend" I mean they kissed in the front row of our local cinema screen for a few months and got drunk round the back of the local pub. And when I say created a new girlfriend, I mean he nicked a picture of somebody's fit cousin and created a profile out of it. It was simple and at the time ingenious and it got him everything he wanted – the girl he longed for got interested in him again, someone in the playground said he'd seen on MySpace that his new girlfriend was "well buff" and he was pretty happy with himself – until his newly restored girlfriend found out the truth. Oh well, life is all about learning curves when you're 14.'

The best social-networking break-up song (although it might also conceivably be the only social-networking break-up song) is Kate Miller-Heidke's excellent *R U F**king Kidding Me*, in which a girl who had her heart broken into tiny pieces by an ex-boyfriend is stunned when, years later, a friend request from him pops up on her social-networking page.

Though it may be very tempting to chart the progress of a painful break-up on a social-networking site, there are several reasons why it might not be the greatest idea:

- When you're suddenly cut off from the person you thought you loved, there's a natural tendency to use your updates as a way of communicating your hurt directly to him or her. So you might say: 'XX is listening to Coldplay and weeping' or 'XX is wondering what's the point in anything' or 'XX is thinking of all the good times and realising she will never feel this way about anyone again.' All heady, sincerely-felt stuff, but it's not exactly going to make the object of your affections say 'Oh, so XX is a snotty, snivelling, desperate, emotional basket-case of a person – I really must get back together with her'. Do you see the problem?

- Posting about how much wrong your ex has done you, and how cruel and barbaric he was and how emotionally stunted, might win everyone else over onto your side. But if you actually get back together with him you're going to have a hell of a lot of explaining to do to the people you've successfully convinced that he is the devil incarnate.

- Your break-up might be the biggest thing that has ever happened to you in your life, and you might well wish to spend days, if not weeks, or months even, analysing every different aspect of your relationship and canvassing for opinion on when things started to go wrong, and sharing each step of your emotional rollercoaster ride, but your friends might just start to get a teensy bit bored. Waking up to ten middle-of-the-night updates of the 'the bottle is the only person you can really trust' variety can soon start to lose its novelty value, and you might find yourself discreetly dropped from people's news feeds.

- Don't forget your audience. When it's 3am and you're listening to *Chasing Cars* for the 150th time, it can be easy to convince yourself you're solely addressing your dear departed ex, which is when the 'Why did you do this to us?' and 'I miss having your body next to mine' updates tend to appear – to the embarrassment of your boss/mother/new friend from the gym, whom you have conveniently forgotten are also able to see your postings.

'DIVORCED – THEN FACEBOOK BROUGHT US BACK TOGETHER'

Mel Dean, 39, divorced her ex-husband Said, 37, nine years ago. She now lives in London with her daughter, Lisa, 7.

'Said and I split up not long after my dad died from lung cancer.

We'd been married for eight years and I hadn't been happy for a long time because I was always the main breadwinner: Said was out of work more than he was in it. But when my dad died, I realised that I couldn't live that way any more. So we split up. It was fairly amicable, we hadn't fallen out of love and neither of us were unfaithful – I just didn't want to support him financially any more.

'We kept in touch for a while but he seemed to disappear off the face of the earth about seven years ago. In the meantime I'd had another relationship which had resulted in my daughter Lisa, although her dad and I couldn't make it work. Then I started my own business so I didn't really think about Said very much for the first few years, but I did wonder. I hoped that things were OK for him, but I didn't know how to find him because I had no idea where he was. And you never know when people seem to disappear, anything could have happened.

'Every now and then I would try to find someone who knew something about him. He'd lived briefly with my sister after we split up so she used to ask around locally. But no one had a clue where he was.

'Last month, I was on the train and I got a Facebook message alert with a Friend Request. The first name was vaguely familiar but I didn't recognise the surname. Then, when I tried to look at the person's picture, I saw the word "Morocco" and I realised it was Said's sister. He's originally from Morocco, so I knew immediately it was about him.

'Before I had a chance to accept the friend request she'd sent me a private message again on Facebook, introducing herself, saying "We're trying to find you". It turned out one of Said's best friends in Morocco, tired of him constantly talking about me, had offered to use Facebook to find me but Said had decided it would be better if his sister got in touch – because he knew I'd recognise the name.

'After a few emails with his sister, we swapped phone numbers and I spoke to Said on the phone. It was so emotional. I couldn't stop crying for two days. I was so happy to know he was alive and well. OK we'd divorced but we'd always been each other's first real love. I was 21 and he was 19 when we got married, we were just kids.

'Two weeks after we spoke, he came to London. He'd been married and divorced and was living in Bordeaux, France, running a patisserie. Now he's planning to sell the business and he might move back here. There's always been love there between us. But I have no idea what will happen in the future, we'll just have to wait and see.

'I still find it incredible to think someone could have tracked me down like that on Facebook. I don't even go on the site that much and I've often thought, "What's the point of it?". But now this has happened I understand that keeping in touch with people around the world IS the point of it, being able to see what's going on in each other's lives. Facebook is definitely a good thing, there's no question of that – used correctly, of course.'

Celebrity Splits

Many stars, used to living in the public gaze, have used social-networking sites to document or publicly announce a break-up.

1. JENNIFER ANISTON & JOHN MAYER

In 2009, Jennifer Aniston called time on her relationship with John Mayer, reportedly after realising he'd been updating his Twitter page every hour, despite claiming he was too busy to stay in regular touch.

Mayer's reaction was, appropriately enough, to tweet about his feelings. 'This heart didn't come with instructions,' was his rueful update following the split.

2. JIM CARREY & JENNY MCCARTHY

Jim Carrey and former love Jenny McCarthy posted news of their April 2010 break-up on their respective Twitter accounts. 'Jenny and I have just ended our 5yr relationship,' the actor wrote. 'I'm grateful 4 the many blessings we've shared and I wish her the very best! S'okay! ?;^>.' Within a half hour of Carrey posting the news, McCarthy too tweeted about their break-up. 'I'm so grateful for the years Jim and I had together. I will stay committed to Jane and will always keep Jim as a leading man in my heart,' she wrote.

3. PRINCE HARRY & CHELSY DAVY

When the royal couple split in January 2009, the news was announced not by a Buckingham Palace spokesperson, but by Chelsy changing her relationship status on Facebook to read 'Relationship: Not in One'. The couple later got back together again before announcing another break-up the following year – not via a social-networking site.

D-I-V-O-R-C-E

Not surprisingly, given the ever-expanding role played by social-networking sites in break-ups, they are also being increasingly implicated in divorce. One firm which specialises in divorce, Divorce-Online, claimed almost one in five petitions they processed cited Facebook. Inappropriate sexual chats, flirty emails and messages were all being put forward as evidence of unreasonable behaviour.

Not only that, divorce lawyers themselves are also using the social-networking sites to gather details of people's dating, social habits and financial status that can later be used as evidence in divorce cases. Divorce-Online also studied over 1,000 divorce petitions produced by the divorce service between 31 December 2009 and 30 June 2010 and found that 102 (10 per cent) of the petitions looked at mentioned Twitter. A closer look at a sample of those petitions revealed that the majority of the errant spouses (72 per cent) were men aged between 35-45 and were earning above £40,000. The common themes in these divorce petitions were that the errant spouse was using Twitter to either conduct affairs or flirt with members of the opposite sex, and their spouses had found out and were using this in their behaviour allegations.

According to figures from the American Academy of Matrimonial Lawyers, (February 2010), 81 per cent of top divorce lawyers in the states have seen an increase in use of evidence gathered from social-networking websites. The sites in question included Facebook, Twitter, MySpace and even business website LinkedIn as well as video-sharing site YouTube.

Facebook is the biggest source of evidence online for divorce lawyers, according to the report, with 66 per cent of divorce lawyers citing the website as the primary source of this sort of evidence. 15 per cent of evidence from online sources comes from MySpace, and just 5 per cent from Twitter.

IN THE PAPERS: 'I FOUND OUT I WAS GETTING A DIVORCE – VIA FACEBOOK!'

Poor Emma Brady, a conference organiser from Accrington, Lancashire, first heard that her husband intended to leave her when a friend rang to console her after reading her husband's latest Facebook post: 'Neil Brady has ended his marriage to Emma Brady'. To make matters worse, when Neil got home from work and his wife asked if he had anything he wanted to say to her, he acted as if nothing had happened. However, not exactly surprisingly, the marriage didn't last…

IN THE PAPERS: 'I FOUND OUT ON FACEBOOK THAT MY "HUSBAND" HAD MARRIED SOMEONE ELSE!'

When Lynn France typed the name of the woman she believed her husband, John, to be having an affair with into the Facebook search box in January 2009, she was looking for clues to confirm her suspicions. What she wasn't expecting was wedding photos of the woman and John getting married at Disney World. Later, he would claim that his marriage to Lynn, who lives in Cleveland, had never been valid, owing to a clerical error. A brief reconciliation between the couple ended when John France flew back to his second 'wife' in Florida taking his and Lynn's two sons with him. During the ensuing legal battle, Lynn was forced to follow her sons' progress from a distance – via photos posted on Facebook.

1. CHERYL COLE

The singer's long-anticipated break-up from ex Ashley Cole was confirmed on Twitter in May 2010 by her PR agent who tweeted: 'We can confirm the divorce. We have no further comment.'

2. KELSEY GRAMMAR

Frasier star, Kelsey Grammar, also chose Twitter as the means of announcing his divorce from third wife Camille Donaticci, writing: 'Hello everyone thank you for ur support and yes it's TRUE Camille and I are divorcing I ask U 2 respect our privacy.' Kelsey nobly appealed to his fans not to take sides. 'I realise that it is human nature but I ask that you be particularly sensitive to the feelings of my wife,' he tweeted later. 'She has been a terrific partner for many years and should not be treated with any disrespect at this time.'

3. DARREN BYFIELD

Walsall striker Darren Byfield tweeted his unhappiness as his split from pop star wife Jamelia deepened into talk of divorce in November 2009. 'By the way it's not good news, so don't get it twisted, night night,' he wrote the night before the divorce was announced. On the day of the announcement he tweeted 'tough times never last but tough people do.' He also tweeted about how much he was looking forward to hearing the chants from rival fans at the next match, such as: 'Where's your Mrs gone? Where's your Mrs gone?'

Revenge is Tweet

Supposing you've been dumped via Bebo or seen photos of your beloved smooching someone else on Facebook, or learned about your own divorce on MySpace. Or supposing you've logged onto Twitter to find out your best friend had a dinner party you weren't invited to or your business partner was actually out shopping that day he pretended to be ill. You're going to be pretty fed up, aren't you? You might even want to get your own back – which is where social-networking sites come in very handy.

For starters, there's the temptation of being able to access someone's entire social network, all in one fell swoop. Then there's also the fact that you're safely hidden behind a computer screen providing a welcome degree of anonymity.

SOME NOTABLE SOCIAL-NETWORKING REVENGE CASES INCLUDE:

1   A scorned woman who got her own back on her ex by messaging all his 445 Facebook friends and branding him a layabout who sponged from the people around him and lazed about all day watching porn. According to the *Sun*, the unidentified woman hacked into the 20-year-old man's account and posted a 582 word rant entitled 'a simple store of sweet revenge'.

2   Martin Tickner who made a bogus Facebook account in the name of his ex-girlfriend and posted explicit photos of her online. The pictures were removed within 24 hours after friends tipped off his ex, and Tickner received a 16-week jail sentence suspended for 12 months and was told to pay £150 costs.

3   Valeria X who was furious when, a few days before her wedding, she saw a photo on her fiancé's Facebook page, showing him in a compromising position with another woman. Determined to get even, she and a friend printed up hundreds of posters and stuck them up in train stations and office blocks around the

Italian city where her fiancé and friends worked. The posters displayed the incriminating photo with the message: 'Thank goodness there's Facebook! At least I've discovered you're a traitor pig before the wedding! Signed, your former betrothed bride and the 548 guests of our wedding.'

4 Cameraman Grant Raphael, who created fake, malicious entries about businessman and old school friend Mathew Firsht after the two had a row. Raphael posted false profiles of Firsht which misrepresented his sexual orientation and his political views and also created a company profile called 'Has Mathew Firsht lied to you?'. Firsht, who runs a company finding audiences for TV shows such as *Big Brother*, sued Raphael for libel and misuse of private information. In April 2009, he was awarded £15,000 for libel and £2000 for breach of privacy. Firsht's company was also awarded £5000 for libel.

You'd think the stars might be above using social-networking sites to get payback. Not a bit of it. It seems that when it comes to revenge, celebrities are just likely to resort to the net as the rest of us.

• In August 2010, teen idol Justin Bieber took revenge on a teenage hacker by posting his telephone number on Twitter and asking his 4.5 million followers to call him. Fellow teenager, Kevin Kristopik was bombarded with calls from Bieber fans after the singer made his number public apparently in retaliation for Kristopik having allegedly hacked into a friend's account to find Bieber's phone number. '@justinbieber is a d**k. (sic)' a furious Kristopik reportedly tweeted. 'i still like him, but this was so low.'(sic).

- Literary figures are also getting in on the act. In June 2009, celebrated novelist Alice Hoffman became so incensed by an underwhelming review of her latest book in the *Boston Globe*, that she retaliated via Twitter. 'Roberta Silman in the *Boston Globe* is a moron,' she tweeted on her page. 'How do some people get to review books? Now any idiot can be a critic.' She also included Silman's phone number and email address and invited her followers to 'tell her what u think of snarky critics.' Philosopher Alain de Botton also resorted to Twitter when wounded by a bad review in the *New York Times*. 'I'm trying out an eye for an eye,' he tweeted, 'the accusation was enormous.'
- Musicians too have proved not adverse to a bit of Revenge-by-Social-networking. In 2009, singer Calvin Harris, stung by a bad review, tweeted his outrage at the prevalence of what he termed 'RICH PEOPLE'S KIDS' in the music industry. Meanwhile, goth idol Marilyn Manson used his MySpace blog to threaten music journalists, after taking offence at a piece in *LA Weekly*.

DO'S AND DON'TS OF SOCIAL-NETWORKING REVENGE

- **DO** make sure it's legal. Listing all the reasons why you think you're a bigger person than your ex isn't likely to end you up in trouble with the law, but making an account in her name and posting intimate photos of the two of you in happier times will.
- **DON'T** try to involve other people. Your mutual friends won't stay mutual for long if you're forever trying to get them to take your side against your ex or your former friend or whomever you perceive has done you wrong.
- **DO** stop to think about how it will look to everyone else. You might think you are completely justified in launching a personal

attack on someone who has upset you, but others might see your behaviour as petty or even unhinged.

- **DON'T** exaggerate. It's human nature to go for the sympathy vote by playing up the other person's 'crimes' as a way of getting revenge, but once you're shown to be being economical with the truth, you'll lose credibility.
- **DO** remember that the best form of revenge is to live life well and be happy.

IN THE PAPERS: CAUGHT IN THE ACT!

Actress Jane Slavin, a big fan of composer Michael Nyman, was initially thrilled when a Facebook message she sent to his fan page led to an invitation out on a date. The two embarked on a heady affair until, inexplicably, Nyman's ardour cooled. In the absence of a proper explanation, Slavin set out to find the truth by creating a Facebook account in the name of a fictional woman, Lucia, complete with beautiful profile picture and sending a fan message to Nyman's Facebook page. The composer responded with a string of flirtatious emails to his gorgeous new admirer, and the two arranged a meeting. When Slavin turned up at the café instead of the glamorous Lucia, Nyman knew he'd been rumbled. After she then went on to tell all to the *Daily Mail*, it's fair to say it was not the most harmonious of endings.

'Would you prefer to make a phone call or update your facebook status ?'

4

Social-Networking Blunders

While social-networking sites can be blamed for some of our online gaffes, there are times when we just have to hold our hands up and admit we messed up all by ourselves.

Caitlynn is now single

(✔Mike likes this)

Mike

woo back on the market. What you doin tonight girl?

Caitlynn

Actually, my boyfriend was hit by a car a few months ago. I just gor aroud to changing my status but im still not over it. Sorry

Jason

nice one, asshole

Don't Forget It's a Public Forum

In the scramble to collect as many online 'friends' as possible and thus spare ourselves the shame and ignominy of being thought unpopular (face it, no one really buys the 'selective' excuse) or in any way a sad, pathetic loser, it's all too easy to forget exactly who is part of your network, and to inadvertently make public knowledge things you really *really* ought to have kept private. A 2009 study for recruiting network Execunet found that 35 per cent of would-be employers found reasons not to hire people based on information gleaned from social-networking sites and the headlines are full of people who have come a cropper because of indiscreet posting:

- When waitress Ashley Johnson from North Carolina complained on her Facebook page that she'd been kept an hour late at the pizza restaurant where she worked by a slow-eating couple who then gave her a lousy $5 tip, she thought she was just harmlessly letting off steam. Unfortunately her bosses didn't see it like that and two days later she was sacked for casting the restaurant in a bad light and disparaging the customers.
- Tenants of a two-bedroom flat in Folkestone, Kent, found themselves facing an eviction order, after their landlady came across photos they'd posted on their Facebook page of wild house parties, complete with guests dancing on the furniture.
- Nathan Singh, a prison officer who worked at HMP Leicester was sacked for gross misconduct after including amongst his Facebook friends 13 current and former inmates, believed to include burglars, fraudsters and someone who'd stabbed another man to death outside a nightclub.
- Hadley Jons couldn't resist posting on her Facebook page her

view that the defendant in an ongoing trial in her home town of Detroit was guilty of resisting arrest. The trouble was, Jons was a juror in the case, and the prosecution hadn't yet finished presenting its evidence. The defence lawyer's son stumbled on the post when looking for a bit of background on the jury and Jons was immediately removed from jury duties.

- Thirteen Virgin Atlantic cabin crew were sacked for bringing the company into disrepute after complaining on their Facebook pages that the passengers were 'chavs' and the planes full of cockroaches

- US fugitive, Maxi Sopo, was busted after posting a series of Facebook updates about how much fun he was having living the high life in the Mexican resort of Cancun.

- 16-year-old Kimberley Swann was sacked after calling her job 'boring', despite not even mentioning the company's name.

- Connor Riley was mortified when, after she tweeted the message, 'Cisco just offered me a job! Now I have to weigh the utility of a fatty paycheck against the daily commute to San Jose and hating the work', she was contacted by a Cisco manager, Tim Levad, who tweeted back 'Who is the hiring manager? I'm sure they would love to know that you will hate the work. We here at Cisco are versed in the web.'

- A group of A&E doctors and nurses from Great Western Hospital in Swindon were suspended in September 2009 for posting photos online of themselves playing The Lying Down Game, a Facebook craze where users post pictures of themselves lying face down with their hands against their sides and their toes pointing downwards. The seven staff members from the A& E department and Acute Assessment Unit posed lying down on resuscitation trollies, ward floors and a heli-pad. They were reinstated the following month.

Status Update

XXX

OMG I HATE MY JOB!! My boss is a total pervvy w***er always making me do shit stuff just to piss me off! W***er!

YYY

Hi XXX, I guess you forgot about adding me on here? Firstly, don't flatter yourself. Secondly, you've worked here 5 months and didn't work out that I'm gay? I know I don't prance around the office like a queen, but it's not exactly a secret. Thirdly, that 'shit stuff' is called your 'job', you know, what I pay you to do. But the fact that you seem able to f**k-up the simplest of tasks might contribute to how you feel about it. And lastly, you also seem to have forgotten that you have 2 weeks left on your 6 month trial period. Don't bother coming in tomorrow. I'll pop your P45 in the post, and you can come in whenever you like to pick up any stuff you've left here. And yes, I'm serious.

There's just something about social-networking sites that seems to encourage users to be, well, less discreet than is good for them. Perhaps it's the fact that we're usually safely shut away in the privacy of our own homes when we access them, so it can be hard to remember that whatever we're writing or posting might reach a wider audience than we'd anticipated.

MY STORY: 'I FORGOT SHE WAS THERE...'

Kiera Cullen, 22, Teaching Assistant

'I remember this awful time I was sitting in front of the TV watching crap telly with all my friends in our shared house in Uni, absent-mindedly checking my Facebook page. We were all chatting away when I noticed this girl pop up on my Facebook chat. A couple of us had been on a weekend trip with her that the Uni organised a few months before and she turned out to be a bit weird so she'd become a bit of a (light-hearted) running joke in the house. I said something to my friends about her popping up and we laughed. Then I noticed another housemate who had also been on that trip had also popped up on Facebook chat so I wrote: 'Hey, come downstairs we're watching TV – also have you noticed so-and-so's online, shall we chat to her haha'. It was supposed to be just a throwaway joke but to my absolute horror I posted it on the weird girl's Facebook chat box instead of my housemate's. It was awful – I actually said HER name to her followed by "haha". As you'd expect she deleted me as a friend pretty quickly after that.'

MY STORY: 'ON SOCIAL-NETWORKING, YOU NEVER KNOW WHERE YOUR PHOTO WILL END UP'

Clare Evans, 20, Administrator

'Whilst at a club in a crowded smoking area I pinched a lighter off the bunch of rowdy partygoers next to me only to find myself (rather involuntarily) in the middle of their group photo. Thinking nothing of it I finished off my cigarette and headed back inside. A couple of weeks later while indulging in a bit of Facebook stalking I had to double take at a photo one of my old school friends had commented on. Staring up from my computer screen was my own face surrounded by a gaggle of complete strangers. The photo was the very same one I had accidentally crashed at the club! She had written below the picture detailing the coincidence. A great use of Facebook finding out all these bizarre connections – but it also means you find yourself having to keep seriously schtum when being introduced to someone for the "first time" when you actually know everything about them from the number of mutual friends they share with you to the fact they love the Arthur theme tune...'

Top Eight Social-networking Gaffes:

1 Jonathan Parker, 19, was convicted of burglary after leaving his Facebook account logged in on his victim's computer, having stopped to check his status before leaving the scene of the crime.

2 President Obama's off-the-record description of rapper Kanye West as a 'jackass' became public knowledge when a staff member at the TV channel where the comments were made tweeted the description on his Twitter page. Though the tweet was hastily deleted, the damage had been done.

3 Kevin Colvin, an intern at Anglo Irish Bank, told his employers he had a family emergency, but his Facebook page revealed he had, in reality, been cavorting in drag at a Halloween party.

4 A Swiss insurance worker told her boss that her headache

prevented her from sitting in front of a computer, but lost her job after she logged into her Facebook account from home. The woman later claimed to have gone online using her iPhone, rather than her PC.

5 In July 2009, Sir John Sawers, the new head of MI6, faced considerable embarrassment after his wife posted family photographs and private details on her Facebook page. Using minimal privacy settings, practically any of the users of the open 'London' network could have had access to information about where the couple live and work, who their friends are and where they go on holiday, with potentially disastrous security implications.

6 In Texas, a driver whose car was involved in a fatal accident found his MySpace postings ('I'm not an alcoholic, I'm a drunkaholic') formed part of the prosecution's case.

7 Arizona businessman, Israel Hyman, thoughtfully treated his 2,000 Twitter followers to a blow-by-blow account of the trip he and his wife were making to Kansas City, with tweets about 'preparing to head out of town' and 'another 10 hours of driving left'. He started to regret being so open about his movements when the couple returned home to find they'd been burgled, with thousands of pounds' worth of electronic equipment stolen.

8 Dmitry Zelenin, a Russian regional governor, became embroiled in his own personal cold war in October 2010 after posting a photo on his Twitter page of a live earthworm on the plate of salad he claimed to have just been served at an official dinner at the Kremlin. 'A salad with live earthworms' was the caption Zelenin used to accompany his picture, and he tweeted that the addition of the worms was a 'very special way to show the salad

was fresh'. It seems President Dmitry Medvedev was not amused, and one of his aides suggested Zelenin should be fired for 'idiocy'. Wonder how he wormed his way out of that one...

More Blunders

Social media sites themselves haven't exactly been exempt from the odd gaffe either. Facebook Beacon, a short-lived feature on the social network that grabbed a user's actions from around the net and reported them back on Facebook, sparked privacy fears almost as soon as it was launched.

Status Update

Kelsea
is in the shower
(✓43 people like this)
Kelsea
seriously guys?

In April 2008, Cathryn Elaine Harris from Texas sued video giant Blockbuster after it used Beacon to share details of her movie rentals with her Facebook friends.

Will X, bought an engagement ring on online retailer site Overstock.com, intending to surprise his girlfriend with a proposal. The romantic gesture was ruined when he saw his purchase broadcast via Beacon to all his friends, including his would-be fiancée.

Not surprisingly, it wasn't long before Facebook closed down Beacon and, under pressure from a class-action lawsuit, proposed to set up a $9.5 million fund to promote the cause of online privacy, safety and security.

Status Update

Alexander

Just finished eating a raw chicken breast, no sweat. Looks like somebody owes me $20

Cale

you're gonna die dude, salmonella for sure

Alexander

I ate chicken, not salmon, dude

Nevertheless, most of us continue to be caught out by social-networking blunders with monotonous regularity, forgetting there's a chance that those drunken photos at last week's party might be viewed by parents, grandparents, prospective employers, teachers and even lawyers.

An American insurance company, defending its refusal to provide health coverage for two minors suffering from eating disorders, tried to include as evidence the contents of litigants' MySpace or Facebook pages to demonstrate that their eating disorders might have 'emotional causes' rather than biological.

Status Update

Charlotte

OMG OMG OMG LEEDS FESTIVAL TOMORROW

Richard

forgot to tell you, I gave your ticket to bella instead

In America, police, colleges and schools are monitoring MySpace and Facebook pages for what they deem to be 'inappropriate' content. Twenty-seven workers at the Automobile Club of Southern California were fired for messages about colleagues on their MySpace sites, a

Florida sheriff's deputy lost his job after his MySpace page revealed his heavy drinking and fascination with female breasts, as did the Argos worker in Wokingham who declared on Facebook that working at the firm was 'shit'. In 2007, two of Britain's most promising young tennis players were suspended by the game's governing body after posting photos and updates on Bebo documenting drunken nights out and hangovers.

So, how can you reduce the risks of compromising social-networking information finding its way into the wrong person's hands?

- Read the social-networking site agreement's small print. A Newport Pagnell man, for instance, was ordered by magistrates not to contact his estranged wife, but when he joined Facebook, an automatic 'friend request' was sent to everyone on his email list, including his former partner. She contacted police; the man was arrested and got 10 days in jail.
- Employ the services of a 'reputation protection' firm to clean up and manage the internet footprint you leave online, burying what's damaging and promoting what's good.
- Always use maximum privacy settings on your account – yes, it might reduce the chances of the love of your life stumbling across your profile page and falling instantly in love with your beauty and wit, but it could also save you a lot of future embarrassment.
- Keep reviewing your privacy settings. The technology on social media sites is constantly evolving, and you need to keep up with it.
- Restrict your friends list to people you actually know and trust.

MY STORY: 'I THOUGHT I KNEW SOMEONE – BUT I'D ONLY SEEN HIS PHOTO ON FACEBOOK!'

Joe Shaw, 21, Waiter

'This is one of those things that happens to everyone all the time – but few people are stupid enough to actually do what I did. I was at a friend-of-a-friend's house, and I didn't really know anyone there except the friend I came with so I was sort of hanging behind them being a bit shy. She was introducing me to everyone and suddenly she introduced me to somebody I recognised. "We've met before" I said, smiling and feeling a little less shy. He didn't seem too sure, and all of a sudden I realised what I'd done – I hadn't met this person before, I'd recognised him off Facebook. I wanted to die. The worst thing is, everybody in the room knew that's what I'd done, because they'd all done it too. It's just they'd been clever enough to realise before it was too late and they said something stupid. So even when I tried to brush it off with – "Oh no, sorry, I'm thinking of someone else", they all knew what I'd done. He also knew what I'd done. I was mortified. So I just got really drunk to get over it.'

'Mum – Get Off My Page!

Few issues are more divisive in modern family life than how much access parents should have to their kids' social-networking accounts – or for that matter, how much parents really want their kids knowing about their own.

> **Status Update**
>
> **Mark**
> AWESOME night. Dry spell = broken
> (✓Karen likes this)
> **Mark**
> MOM WTF
> **Karen**
> oops. How do I unclick?

SCHOOL-AGE KIDS

When a May 2010 survey for National Family Week found that well over a quarter of young people rated Facebook as having more influence over them than money, health, sports, pets, school and even parents, there was universal outcry. The study of 3,000 parents and 1,000 children found that kids living in single-parent homes with just a mum found Facebook most important with 62 per cent ranking it their main influence, as compared to one in ten living with their dad and seven per cent living with both parents thinking this.

If social-networking is that important to our kids, surely we should insist on being part of the whole experience? That's the big dilemma parents are facing, made doubly difficult by the fact that most children and teens would rather eat cabbage and floss nightly than include their parents among their thousand or so friends. So aghast are they that there's even a website, myparentsjoinedfacebook.com, where people post screen views of their parents' most embarrassing posts.

Bonnie K

is sick of being fat and happy, so were going to the gym so I can be skinny and miserable... but at least ill be skinny

Samuel

Or you could come and train with me. I'm on my old training regime again.

Caroline

Me too! Which gym?

Jim K

FAT...YOU??!!!??? No way Babe. I'll shoot anyone who says different!!! I've heard that a good sex session is the equivalent to a marathon re burning off the fat. Take up running and let Matt run the Marathons!!!

Bonnie K

ummm dad... ew don't ever say that stuff ever again!!!

A Nielsen survey in August 2010 found that three quarters of parents said they were friends with their children on Facebook, with 41 per cent making it a house rule that their children had to add them as friends. However nearly 30 per cent of teens said they would unfriend their parents if given the choice, being more than twice as likely to want to unfriend their mother than their father. In nearly half of cases, children said they would prefer to be friends with their parents privately on the web without their parents having the ability to post comments.

Nielsen questioned 1,024 parents and 500 children aged 13 to 17 for the online poll. More than half of the youngsters admitted they don't personally know all of their Facebook friends, and 41 per cent of parents said they knew half or less of their children's Facebook friends. A fifth of parents admitted they had told their children to unfriend someone.

5 REASONS NOT TO 'FRIEND' YOUR KIDS ON FACEBOOK:

1 You will find out far more than you want to know about their sex lives.
2 You will see photos of the wild house party that took place *at your house* that night you were away visiting Grandma.
3 You will suddenly realise what exactly happened to the toilet brush that went missing that night.
4 Your kids will see shameful photos of you dancing drunkenly at your work Christmas party.
5 They will think it hysterical to hack into your account (everyone knows people over forty have the same password for everything – quite often their own name) and update your status to 'XX just farted'.

5 REASONS NOT TO 'FRIEND' YOUR PARENTS ON FACEBOOK:

1 They will post messages on your wall about verruca appointments and warn that your newest friend might be a paedophile masquerading as a 13-year-old.
2 They will post comments on your photos and attempt to be funny.
3 They will 'friend' some of your friends who will be too embarrassed to say no.
4 They will think it cute to tag you in naked baby pix.
5 They will correct your spelling and grammar.

Things have become so tricky regarding the parents/children Facebook relationship that Stanford University in California has even started offering courses on 'Facebook for Parents', created by B J Fogg, who also runs a website facebookforparents.org which guides parents through the minefield of children's social-networking habits.

Parents' fears about the practice won't have been assuaged by the warnings of top scientist, Susan Greenfield, a neuroscientist at Oxford University, about how social-networking sites like Facebook, Twitter and Bebo are in effect 're-wiring' young people's brains, shortening attention spans, encouraging instant gratification and making them more self-centred. Scary stuff when you consider a study by the Broadcaster Audience Research Board found teenagers now spend an average of seven-and-a-half hours a day in front of a screen.

Jason   Status Update
My grampa just got promoted to level 36 in mafia wars. Cool...

Psychologist Dr Aric Sigman believes there is a case for parents to have access to their children's social-networking pages, but not usually the other way around.

'Given what is happening with social-networking, looking at each other's Facebook pages is a variation on having access to each other's diaries.

'Certainly, for younger children, it's important that parents do know what is going on. But there's no reason why children, if they're younger, should have access to your Facebook page. The Facebook page for adults can be for adults. I don't think there should be equal rights at all. Until children move out of the house, there shouldn't be equal rights. Social-networking is one of many areas where parents should always have more power than children.'

For social psychologist Dr Arthur Cassidy it's a question of protection. 'Where minors are concerned, parents have a duty of care to children. At the same time it should be done in a fairly discreet, tentative way that won't harm the relationship with the child.

'Saying "You're banned from Facebook" isn't the right way to go about it – it can be psychologically destructive and it can frighten a child, particularly if it doesn't come with an explanation.

'Depending on the age of a child, it's better for parents to take the child into their confidence about social-networking and to talk to them about it, explaining which form of making friends is good and which isn't.

'Most social-networking sites have protective features but they are not watertight. Cyber fraudsters or predators can work round it on Facebook, which is why we have problems.

'So parents can do a certain amount to allow their kids to enjoy Facebook by teaching them how not to put personal information on it – and how to follow the basic rules of social networking the basic rules of social-networking.'

Status Update

Kadison M
I'm Sick of Being Treated Like A Baby I Have My Own Life JUST LET ME DRINK

Timm M
Settle down kaddie. It's worth waiting for.:)

> **Kadison M**
> ummmmm and who are you
> **Timm M**
> Your uncle... haven't seen you in nearly 10 years though

OLDER KIDS

The water can get even murkier when it comes to older children. So-called 'helicopter parents' who hover over their children's lives even after they've left home are using social-networking sites to keep tabs on their offspring from afar. According to a September 2010 poll commissioned by insurance company Ensleigh, three quarters of parents use Facebook to check up on children who have left home for university. However only one third of students wanted to be Facebook friends with their parents, with nearly three quarters putting their reluctance down to not wanting their mums and dads to see personal pictures or messages. The poll found that three quarters of parents believe the latest technologies make it easier for them to keep in touch with their student children during term time.

An earlier poll by the Department of Innovation, Universities and Skills revealed that 23 per cent of parents use social-networking as their main way of contacting their children. The survey found that parents living in Worcester have taken social-networking most to their hearts, with 83 per cent becoming 'friends' with their student children in order to stay in touch, compared with only a third (33 per cent) of parents from Bristol.

For many parents it's a convenient way of staying in contact with children hell-bent on stretching their wings, but there's plenty of anecdotal evidence that the online 'friends' relationship can be fraught with problems. Common areas of conflict include:

- Parents who reduce their offsprings' allowance, or even cut it altogether, after seeing photographic evidence of their high-living ways on social-networking sites.
- Parents snooping on their children's friends, trying to vet them.

SHOULD PARENTS BE 'FRIENDS' WITH THEIR CHILDREN ON FACEBOOK: THE EXPERTS SPEAK

FOR

Dr David Smallwood, an independent addiction counsellor and psychotherapist, believes that despite the inevitable objections it will raise, it's a good idea for parents to keep an eye on what their children are doing on social-networking sites.

'Yes it is advisable. If your kid is a 15-year-old social networker, you need access to their pages in the interests of transparency and knowing what they are up to. And you can't have one rule for them and another for yourself, so the whole thing has to be open and transparent, with them being able to access your pages too.'

Dr Smallwood also recommends regulating the amount of time children spend social-networking. 'The problems can start, or be worrying, if the length of time a child spends on a site is excessive. Half an hour a day is fine. Three hours a day is far too excessive; that's three hours where they're not interacting with others.'

And don't listen to any arguments about social-networking being the same as social interaction.

'While it's about other people, it's not real, it's fantasy. Yes it's real people and real information, but often people go into a cyber-world without fully understanding that it's not the real world; people don't talk to each other in the same way as they do in the real world.'

As an adult, allowing your children to access your own private web pages can be tricky, and it can be difficult to decide – or even agree – on boundaries of what it is acceptable for them to discuss. No parent really wants their 14-year-old chiming in on a post about sex. But making sure that children have a clear idea of what is and isn't acceptable for them to share on a social-networking page is fraught with problems.

'It's a minefield,' says Dr Smallwood. 'How do you set out everything you don't want them to look at? Social-networking is geared towards encouraging people to disclose information that they might not give out in another context. You are in a cyberworld – it's the world, but it's not. It's almost as if you are looking at what is happening through frosted glass, rather than having the clarity of what is really happening.'

Not being able to see the people they're connecting with in person, often leaves children feeling socially unmoored, not sure of the appropriate reaction.

'For example, how is it we know whether someone is angry with us or not?' asks Dr Smallwood. 'The easy way is to watch their body language, listen to their tone of voice, watch their facial expression. But there's none of this on Facebook. And kids are often disinhibited, they'll sometimes write anything down. Which can be a real problem.'

AGAINST
'It's about balance,' says psychologist Dr Karol Szlichinski. 'Parents have to balance the issue of safeguarding their children from internet

predators against a teenager's need to develop a life separate from their parents and have a normal life with their own friends and social group.

'So they have to get the balance right, depending on the age of the child, and the degree of trust the parents have in the relationship. With small children, parents should be monitoring, in general, what goes on on the internet. But with teenagers it's more about keeping the lines of communication open and talking about issues like drugs, sex and meeting weirdos on the internet.

'I'm not sure monitoring a teenager's social network pages is the best way of maintaining trust. It would be better to talk to them about it rather than tracking their social network usage.

'When it comes to children accessing parents' pages on sites, it depends on what the parents are using social networks for. If, for instance, it's just to keep other family members in touch by putting up holiday snaps, there are no problems with children seeing that: you'd expect them to want to.

'But if, for example, the parent is looking for a new partner, that's a rather different issue. The same kind of thinking should apply as if they are dating new partners face to face – parents should try to keep communication open and talk developments over with their children, but not necessarily online.

'Similarly, some people lead fantasy lives on social-networking sites which stay firmly in the realms of fantasy. They might discuss meeting up with someone romantically on a site – but have no intention of doing so. If children find out about that via a site, it could be fairly damaging or disruptive. You have to be quite sophisticated to know when a fantasy life is just fantasy and there can't be many circumstances in which it would be appropriate to share that with a child.'

MY STORY: 'I ACCIDENTALLY "FRIENDED" MY CHILDREN'S FRIENDS!'

Michael Scott, 53, Solicitor

'I only created a Facebook [page] because my daughter went to university and stopped picking up our calls. I'd email or text her about money or something else and just would never get a reply. The only way I thought she might actually get back to me was Facebook. So I started up an account and added her. Of course this mortified her but she accepted and got a little better at getting back to me. My son and his best friend were round the house one day when my son's friend noticed me checking Facebook on the laptop. "I didn't know you had Facebook!" he said. "Here, let me help you add everybody." Now, at this point my only two friends were my son and my daughter. So when he went to add everybody what he actually meant was add all the "you may know" people – all my children's friends, who I didn't know at all. It was very embarrassing, especially as I didn't really realise he had done it till my daughter enquired as to why I was friends with half her old classmates from secondary school. I've since deleted everybody, including my son and daughter, just be to safe.'

MY STORY: 'CAUGHT OUT – BY HER DAD!'

Oscar Phillips, 19, student

'There was this one time I put up photos on a friend's Facebook while we were watching TV. They were just pictures of the night before taken on his phone. We'd gone out in central London and ended up pretty drunk in a place in Soho. It had been a really good night, and the photos were quite funny because he was obviously drunk by the time he took them – I always find that people only remember they have a camera on them or that their phone takes pictures halfway through the night when everybody's really drunk, looks terrible, and can't hold the camera straight. Anyway, I put them up, closed the laptop and sort of forgot about them. A couple of hours later, we got a frantic call from a friend; he was talking so fast it took us a minute to work out what exactly he was saying. Turns out, we hadn't been looking closely enough at the photos. He directed us to one of them, a picture of him and his girlfriend. I flicked through and found it and burst out laughing. At the time the club had been so dark, and we were all wearing our beer goggles, so no one had noticed that his poor girlfriend's top had come completely undone. Worse still is that, of all the people, it was her dad who spotted she'd been tagged and called to alert her! Really shows you should never be friends with your parents on Facebook...'

Defriending a Parent

If you think becoming online friends with your parent or child is tricky, try becoming non-friends. Being defriended by a close family member can feel like a major rejection.

Is there a 'nice' way of telling your mum you no longer want to be her 'friend'? Probably not, which is why most kids don't even tell their parents they've been defriended, leaving them to find out the unpalatable truth for themselves when they log in and find themselves locked out of their children's profile page.

'The only way to talk around it is to talk through what is really going on,' advises Dr Karol Szlichinski, a psychologist specialising in new technology. But even that, it seems is age-dependent.

'A 17-year-old, living at home, who has been using social-networking for some time, might be able to explain it properly by saying, "I'm older now and I'd like to lead my own life, it's time I started separating social and family life".

'But it's still a difficult conversation for a teenager, even though in principle it's part of the normal separation process that happens as teens grow up. And a 13-year-old wouldn't have the language to say that it was part of manifesting separation.'

Dr Arthur Cassidy, a social psychologist, agrees that defriending can actually be a healthy demonstration that a child is pushing for more independence. 'It means they want to be in control of their own leisure time. They isolate the parents because they feel the parents are a problem. Defriending is the child's way of removing the parent to create their own sense of autonomy.'

Instead of keeping tabs on their social-networking pages, parents can help their children negotiate the minefield of online interaction in different ways, says Dr Cassidy.

'We need to educate parents to understand how to deal with children's coping mechanisms for networking – and for parents themselves to know how to cope. It works both ways. Children fall out with each other over bullying on networking sites, for instance. But they don't know how to tell their parents.

'Some can articulate it and say "so-and-so made me cry". But they might not use the word "bullying". We need a much more stringent approach on how parents deal with this – and to know how to look for the signs of online predators. Even parents who are very advanced with computing itself may not know how to deal with this specific area – and how to alert their kids to fake identities.'

Other experts take a tougher stance on the defriending issue. 'I am a hard liner for authority and parents being respected,' says Dr Aric Sigman. 'I don't like the idea of a child saying "I'm defriending you". They're being disrespectful to their parents, unless it's not being done with a teenage sense of irony. It's a virtual version of closing the door and sulking in their room.'

Even worse would be if the situation was reversed. 'If a parent defriends a child, that would be very damaging,' says Dr Sigman.

Safety

Civilisation has taken centuries to evolve laws for interaction within society to keep civilians safe, but online social interaction is a new phenomenon and we're still coming to terms with the safety implications. Dangers range from the physical – people you encounter online but who then infiltrate your 'real' life – to the psychological. Users have complained of cyber-stalking, cyber-bullying and online abuse.

CHILD SAFETY

It used to be said that the telly was the best babysitter, but now that honour must surely go to the computer screen. Thanks to social-networking, kids and young people can while away hours chatting and interacting online from the safety of their own homes. Well, that's the theory anyway. In reality, social-networking can be just as dodgy as interacting out in the real world. Not only are there the predators posing as other children and teenagers, hoping to lure a child into a face-to-face meeting (the existence of whom, luckily, most children now seem very aware of), there are also bullies and people trying to sell stuff or steal identities or gatecrash parties they weren't invited to.

The Childline website warns children not to use their real names or give away personal information, such as addresses or phone numbers, or to post any photos or videos they wouldn't be happy for their teachers or parents to see. It also advises them not to tell anyone their password, even their best friend, and not to forget that anything they post can be copied or re-posted, even if they later try to delete it.

In February 2010, the European Commission assessed 22 social-networking sites and found that more than half of them had default settings which failed to hide the personal details of under-18s. It reported that just 40 per cent of the sites they examined had default settings which hid the personal information of minors from all but their friends and family, and just 11 of the 22 sites examined stopped minors' profiles being visible to search engines.

IN THE PAPERS: CYBER-BULLYING TRAGEDY

Worried that her daughter was being victimised by her 13-year-old friend, Lori Drew and a young accomplice decided to create a fake MySpace account in the name of a fictitious 16-year-old boy to find out what the girl was saying. But the Missouri mum's plans took on a life of their own when the 13-year-old girl at the centre of their hoax ended up killing herself after the fake 16-year-old systematically undermined her, finally telling her the world would be a better place without her. The case caused worldwide controversy when Drew was convicted in 2008 of unauthorised access to computers for violating MySpace's terms of service. However, the conviction was overturned the following year.

5 WAYS TO USE FACEBOOK MORE SAFELY

Psychologist Dr Arthur Cassidy advises:

1 For your psychological safety, make a conscious effort to replace most of your Facebook time with real social interaction, such as seeing people face to face and going out and about to socialise. Even talking on the phone is an improvement on spending most of your time online in front of a screen.

2 Be very aware – and talk to other Facebook friends to encourage their awareness too – that cyber-criminals can operate on social-networking sites. You don't have to be alarmist – making it a rule not to reveal personal information at any time is a good way to keep yourself safe from any criminal activity.

3 Refuse to comply with any requests about information about your life and become more skilled at learning more about internet safety.

4 Never accept Facebook invitations to parties unless you have already met the people involved.

5 Keep your Facebook contacts to a minimum. Having too many causes loss of control – and only encourages you to divulge personal information.

Common Sense and Nonsense

The real problem with social-networking is that it's so new that we're all still working out the rules as we go along, and there's a tendency to imagine that we won't know exactly how to conduct ourselves as we're still learning. However, much of staying safe and healthy and happy online comes down to common sense.

DR ARTHUR CASSIDY'S 10 BASIC RULES OF SOCIAL-NETWORKING

1 THINK before you reveal any personal information on any social-networking site – even things like your date of birth can be used in identity fraud.

2 IF someone does not want to be your friend, be polite and courteous – arguing or becoming abusive is not a good idea.

3 LEARN how to deal with Facebook bullies. Bullies love social-networking sites; they're everywhere. Be more assertive, not by challenging them, but by blocking and ignoring them.

4 LEARN how to spot the signs of cyber criminals: patterns of 'cool' language that your friends or peer group never ever use is one big giveaway.

5 INFORM the police if you think someone is using a fake identity or is an adult predator in disguise as a teenager.

6 AVOID talking about emotionally laden or sexual matters of any description to friends or anyone else on networking sites – no matter how strongly you might feel at the time.

7 NEVER open any links or attachments unless you have met the sender.

8 NEVER divulge your password to anyone. Change it frequently.

9 BE very aware that every photo has the potential to be a false identity – with a fake profile.

10 LIMIT your hours on social-networking. Use it mostly for getting reliable and up-to-date knowledge about a range of topics.

Social-networking – Office Politics

If you work in the kind of company which favours team-building exercises and open-plan layouts, and where even the boss sportingly makes a tea round on a Friday afternoon, it can be tempting to add all your workmates to your friends and followers lists, regardless of rank or likeability. But before you press the 'accept' box, you should consider carefully the pros and cons of mixing business with social-networking pleasure.

PROS
- You'll get to know your colleagues better, and find common interests.
- You'll have a hotline to your boss.
- You'll have another tool for work networking.

CONS
- You'll have to constantly vet your photos, even the ones where you're tagged by other people.
- You can never complain about work, even in a 'Thank God it's Friday' way.
- Your colleagues/boss will be able to monitor exactly when you're logging on – during office hours, sick days, or when you're supposed to be working at home.

The trouble is that even if you decide sharing the intimate details of your private life with the entire management team isn't the best idea in the world, you're still stuck with the delicate issue of how to decline a friend request, particularly if the person making it pays your salary! A survey carried out in April 2010 by IT security company F-Secure, found that a massive 73 per cent of respondents avoided 'friending' their manager on Facebook.

WORKFRIENDS.COM – SOCIAL-NETWORKING ETIQUETTE DO'S AND DON'TS

- **DON'T** invite your boss to be 'friends'. Wait for the invitation to come from him or her, otherwise it might put them in an awkward position.
- **DO** constantly monitor your online profile, making sure there's nothing remotely incriminating (what's known as 'cleaning up your digital dirt').
- **DON'T** be afraid to discreetly adjust your privacy settings if you're worried, so that you are still 'friends' but restrict who has access to comments on your wall or photos of you.
- **DO** bear in mind that even if your current employers are relaxed about what appears on your social-networking page, future potential employers might not be and you might be ruling yourself out of a job.

Before you dismiss the idea of superpoking the boss out of hand, bear in mind research carried out by IBM and MIT, which tracked the electronic communication of 7,000 people over a three-year period, found that having strong internet-based connections to managers added up to an extra £365 in extra revenue a month.

Some employers, however, aren't so keen on mixing social-networking with the workplace. A survey of 1,000 executives from 17 countries including the UK, by computer antivirus company McAfee, found that nearly half the companies surveyed had banned the use of Facebook during work hours, and about a quarter of companies monitored employee use of social media sites for inappropriate behaviour.

A separate survey of 1,460 office workers published in October 2009 by IT company Morse, claimed that 57 per cent of workers were accessing social-networking sites for personal use during work hours, spending an average of 40 minutes a week, at a cost to business of £1.38billion each year. It had previously emerged that Portsmouth City Council specifically banned staff from using Facebook, after discovering workers were spending a total of 413 hours a month on the website, and Hillingdon Council reportedly drew up a code of conduct for staff, limiting their Twitter time.

In October 2010 the *Mail on Sunday* revealed that Government departments and quangos, including officials planning the 2012 Olympics, were also coming down hard on workers' social-networking during office hours. The paper also claimed they were paying thousands of pounds to outside consultants to run courses on the do's and don'ts of how to behave on Facebook and similar sites and on the need to protect sensitive data from becoming public. Staff were reportedly told they could use social-networking sites in their lunch breaks, but not to publish content about London 2012.

Meanwhile Cheshire Constabulary imposed a total ban on social-networking from work computers unless for police business, and both Rochdale Borough Council and St Helens Borough Council admitted having disciplined staff for posting on social-networking sites while supposedly off sick.

MY STORY: 'I ACCIDENTALLY LEFT MY FACEBOOK PAGE ON IN THE OFFICE...'

Kitty Lewis Williams, 25, Gallery Assistant

'Like everybody else I have a love/hate relationship with Facebook – you wish you could delete and yet you can't keep away from it, it's an ongoing cycle and it's a losing battle. When I left university I was unemployed and on Facebook a lot, because it was either that or trawling through job sites, so occasionally you wander. When I finally got something it was dull as anything and paid terribly but nonetheless it was (some) money so I got on with it. Facebook, like any other addiction, is tough to kick and although I wasn't at home on the sofa job hunting, I was in a stuffy office with not much to do and had a computer, so it was quite easy to get a quick fix every hour or so. Like with all things that are boring, you get more and more careless as time goes on. It was stupid but not unusual for me to write on a friend's wall while at work something like "PLEASE SAVE ME FROM THIS DULL, DULL HELL" – of course it took one post-delivery person to get stuck trying to open the door, one distraction for me to leave my desk with those words written on the screen, and it was all over. Well, not really. My supervisor saw, that's for sure, but instead of saying or doing anything she was just that little bit more nasty to me. She made sure it was only me that noticed. She was subtle. Stuff like stealing my stapler. Thank God I quit after a couple of months. And learnt never to check Facebook on a work computer.'

IN THE PAPERS: A CAUTIONARY TALE

Kyle Doyle had reason to rue the day he made his manager his Facebook friend. The Australian call-centre worker was incensed when, after calling in sick, his manager sent him an email requesting a doctor's certificate. Doyle emailed back insisting he was on leave for medical reasons. 'You cannot deny leave based on a line manager's discretion, with no proof,' he wrote. The manager's reply was brief: 'I believe the proof that you are after is below'. Pasted underneath was a screenshot of Doyle's Facebook update from the day in question: 'not going to work, f... it i'm still trashed. SICKIE WOO!' Oops.

The increasingly blurred social-networking lines between work and pleasure were behind a suggested German draft law to make it illegal for prospective employers to spy on applicants' private postings. Some German companies had caused outrage by checking on employee emails and filming sales clerks during coffee breaks. The vetting of would-be employees' private social-networking sites was seen as an intrusion too far.

MIXING WORK WITH SOCIAL-NETWORKING PLEASURE: THE EXPERTS SPEAK...

'Some people like to bring family and work-life close,' says psychologist Dr Karol Szlichinski. 'But there's always a risk in blurring work/home boundaries – particularly if there is something unusual about your personal life. There's a risk of information getting into the work environment that you really don't want to get in there.

'You have to be extremely careful about what you say. If you want to gripe about the people at work or your horrible job, you shouldn't let work colleagues into your network.

'In the recruitment process nowadays, there's more emphasis not just on your ability but your attitude, what sort of frame of mind you bring to the workplace. The temptation in this situation is to present yourself, quite casually, to a prospective employer as someone who uses social networks sometimes, saying for example: "Oh I may just sound off on Facebook on Friday night after a few beers".

'You could easily live to regret those words. Because if the boss too is on Facebook, it's out there. It's the same kind of thing as avoiding situations where you get drunk with the boss and say the wrong thing. You don't go there.'

Social psychologist Dr Arthur Cassidy is similarly dubious. 'You are creating a very intense environment if you bring work and social-networking together. It means you are opening up your private life, sharing yourself and your thoughts about the work environment with other people in the same environment.

'This can jeopardise your own position, particularly if you share with your boss or line manager. You could be shooting yourself in the foot.'

5

Friends Online and Petworking

Friends – General Rules

Once upon a time, friends were people you shared common interests or history with, who supported you when things got tough, and, most crucially, who you met in person, or at least spoke to on the phone often enough to at least recognise their voice. Mark Vernon, author of *The Philosophy of Friendship*, estimates that the average person needs between six and twelve close friends who meet the above criteria. However, social-networking has changed all that.

XX   Status Update

We celebrated your birthday by going to Olive Garden for lunch. Too bad you weren't there!

YY

uhhhhhhh... Thanks?

To become someone's friend on a social-networking site, you don't have to communicate with them regularly, you don't have to share common ground, you don't even have to know them. Often it's enough just to have stumbled across one another on cyberspace. Friendships that used to be forged over an extended period of time can now be entered into in the space of a click of a mouse. Young people in particular seem to view the collection of online friends as a full-time job, and anyone boasting fewer than 500 risks being seen as a bit of a loner. American comedian Steve Hofstetter is believed to hold the record for the most popular social networker, amassing 400,000 friends on MySpace and 200,000 on Facebook, before the site set a limit of 5,000.

However, the average number of Facebook friends is a mere 120, which closer concurs with what experts believe is the maximum we can fully cope with. Robin Dunbar, Professor of Evolutionary Anthropology at Oxford University, developed the theory of 'Dunbar's Number' in the 1990s, before the advent of online social-networking. According to the theory, the size of our neocortex – the part of the brain used for conscious thought and language – limits the number of 'friends' we are capable of managing to 150. Dunbar defined 'friend' as someone you care about and contact at least once a year.

Our 'friends' network usually consists of an inner circle of five 'core' people and an additional layer of ten, some of whom might be family members. This is your central group and then, outside that, there are another 35 in the next circle and another 100 on the outside. This is the extent of the social world our brains can cope with. Even when social network users list thousands of friends, researchers examining traffic on profile pages found that the same inner circle of 150 tended to be maintained.

Yet for many social network site devotees, bigger is definitely better and friends' lists running into the thousands are almost the norm among the under-25s, all of which has given rise to another phenomenon: friendship addiction.

In 2008, David Smallwood, an addictions expert, warned that women, whose self-worth tends to stem from relationships with others and who are better at maintaining friendships, whether cyber or 'real', were particularly at risk of developing a compulsion towards acquiring friends. According to Dr Smallwood, at least 10 per cent of the population were vulnerable to 'friendship addiction'.

YOU KNOW YOU'RE SUFFERING FROM 'FRIENDSHIP ADDICTION' WHEN:

1 You judge yourself by how many online friends you have.
2 You believe people with more friends than you are more popular.
3 You regularly comb through your friends' friends' lists for people to add to your own.
4 The first thing you do when you get home from a party is add all the people you just met as friends.
5 You have at least 20 people on your friends' list that you actively dislike.

Adding random people as friends might provide an illusion of popularity, but it has two major drawbacks: a) you lose track of who can see your profile, which leaves you more exposed to social faux pas, and b) you run the risk of your friendship request being ignored, which can lead to feelings of rejection and inadequacy.

Little wonder, the 18 – 34-year-olds have been dubbed the 'Eleanor Rigby generation', concentrating on virtual communication at the expense of real social interaction. Not only does that lead to feelings of loneliness, it also does nothing to replenish levels of the so-called 'cuddle hormone' oxytocin, vital to wellbeing and boosted by actual physical contact.

The Archbishop of Westminster, Vincent Nichols, warned that social-networking sites were also having a negative effect on society's ability to build communities and were leading young people to seek out 'transient' friendships, with an emphasis on quantity rather than quality.

Psychologist Dr Aric Sigman believes that there are serious drawbacks to having hundreds of online friends. 'There's a new kind of social competitiveness and it makes you feel "popular" in the virtual sense, but there's a grey dividing line between virtual and real friends and the people who don't recognise this do have a problem.'

Investing time in cultivating online friendships could be detrimental to someone's ability to conduct friendships in real life, warns Dr Sigman.

'Spending a lot of time, when young, doing this is not good for mental or physical development. It's the latest thing that is displacing people from having a REAL conversation; yet there's a medical, emotional and social need for people to have REAL friends, that they see face to face frequently. Anything that threatens that has to be looked at very carefully.'

Social psychologist Dr Arthur Cassidy agrees that amassing friends on social network sites can get in the way of establishing real and meaningful friendships. 'It's natural to want to have friends but this is about reinforcing the idea of friendship, so it snowballs. By creating so many friends, in fact you are creating social distance because you couldn't possibly have time to have any form of meaningful relationship with so many people. All you really have is an electronic relationship with a microchip. You are interacting with a microchip.

'We are also destroying the language of real communication by using this electronic communication to interact with our friends. We are becoming more deficient in our social and language skills because of this.'

WHEN LESS IS MORE

A study of 70 students at a college in Massachusetts found a correlation between the number of Facebook friends and undergraduate social adjustment. First-year students with 200 or more friends were found to have lower levels of self-esteem and to struggle more with personal and academic adjustment than those with less than 200 friends. In other words, the more online friends, the fewer actual friends. However the discrepancy wore off over time and by the end of university, students with more than 200 friends scored higher levels of social adjustment.

SOME INTERESTING FACTS ABOUT ONLINE FRIENDS

In February 2010, a Railcard survey of 1,000 people uncovered some surprising friendship facts:

- One third of Facebook users boast more than 170 online friends, but nearly 60 per cent of them admitted they meet regularly with only ten of them.

- 78 per cent of 51 – 55-year-olds (who each have an average of 31 friends) saw five or less friends in person each month.
- 16 – 18-year-olds met up with an average of 12 of their online friends at least once a month.
- 41 per cent blamed time restrictions as the main reason for not meeting up with their online friends more often, with 27 per cent opting for distance instead.

The 5 Worst Types of Facebook Friend

1. THE SHOW-OFF

He doesn't want friends so much as an admiring audience. Every update, every photo, every Scrabble move even, is designed to demonstrate his superiority over you and with the express aim of making you covet his life. This kind of friend will just make you feel bad about your own existence.

2. THE GUILT-TRIPPER

Every time you post a photo of you with friends, or a comment about somewhere you've visited, or a social event you enjoyed, you are guaranteed to get a doleful comment. 'Oh, looks like you had fun, wish you'd let me know…', 'Wow – you went to Italy! All I managed was a week in the caravan in Dorset. And it rained every day'. 'I didn't know X and Y were coming with you – didn't you say it was just a small thing?' Soon you won't dare put anything up for fear of the guilt fallout afterwards.

3. THE NIT-PICKER

You didn't technically meet Tony Blair, you just stood in the queue and watched the back of his head while he signed his book. That photo of you running in the Race for Life might *look* like you're approaching the finish, but actually it was taken when you weren't even halfway through. The party wasn't *that* good to be fair... Recognise this type of comment? Bad luck, because it means you've been lumbered with a nit-picker friend, someone who sees it as their mission in life to correct you online, in front of all your friends and colleagues.

4. THE SPIRITUAL LEADER

You might not be concerned about the state of your chakras, but your friend certainly is. So much so that she doesn't desist in sending you comments and updates designed to lead you onto a higher spiritual plane. Either that or they send you completely round the twist. 'Don't forget that the universe is bountiful and give thanks for the boundless joy that surrounds you,' she might tell you first thing on a rainy Monday morning. 'All setbacks are just ways of helping us to grow and learn to love' she will inform you when you complain about your train being late. She might be right. But it doesn't make you feel better. It just makes you cross.

5. THE BAD INFLUENCE

'Just about to nip out for a quick Friday lunchtime pint. See you in the Queens? 20 minutes?'

   'No can do. Working flat out, deadline at 5pm.'

   'Just a half then. Won't kill you will it? I'm buying.'

   'Absolutely not. I'm a day late as it is.'

'Well, an extra 20 minutes isn't going to make much difference then, is it? Come on, we're all going. Don't be a spoilsport. You know you want to.'

In reality, you know you don't want to. You know you don't want anything less than you want to go out drinking in the middle of a busy Friday. But you're on a social-networking site, and other people are seeing this exchange and forming opinions about how straight-laced and boring you are. Plus, all your other friends who are going are now ganging up on you to come. Maybe just one then…

A FACEBOOK FRIEND TOO FAR

An American undergraduate who was hauled up in front of his university disciplinary board following an altercation with an off-duty policeman and threatened with expulsion, filed a lawsuit against the university after discovering that one of the members of the disciplinary panel was Facebook friends with the policeman. Even though the panel member had over 400 Facebook friends and insisted it didn't qualify as a 'real' friendship, the court found there had been a 'procedural defect'.

Ask The Experts: Is Social-networking Undermining Real Friendship?

YES:

Dr David Smallwood, independent addiction counsellor and psychotherapist, believes that when it comes to online networking friends, people often mistake quantity for quality:

'If I have 150 friends and you have 50, there's a tendency to think that makes me "better" than you; it's pure one-upmanship.

'If you feel a bit "less than", sometimes having someone there to put their arm around you and make you feel better fixes that feeling. So people believe the more friends they have, the better it will be.'

Unfortunately, it doesn't work that way. And the more friends you have, the more chance there is that you'll end up suffering from that scourge of the Facebook generation: Friends Envy.

'People put: "I've just bought a new VW Golf" on Twitter. So if you can't afford a new VW Golf, you're going to feel less than adequate,' says Dr Smallwood. This kind of thing is, in simplest terms, a perfect marketing tool: creating envy.

'Moreover, social-networking devalues friendships because real friendships can actually be gauged by looking at a person, and from doing something for each other, not for gain but for the sake of the friendship itself.

'In order for a friend to behave as a friend and be a friend you need to be able to form the friendship on a one-to-one basis; the real way of doing it. And you form those strong relationships with a small number of people – if you're lucky. In reality, if you were servicing 100 real friends, you wouldn't have time for anything else, would you?'

NO

Psychologist Dr Karol Szlichinski says: 'People have lots of online friends because they like to feel connected and popular. And possibly it's a "collecting" thing for some people.

'If you run a PR company, you want to know thousands of people. Some people have perfectly good professional reasons for wanting that number of contacts. And contact with different people in different walks of life in other countries can certainly be enriching – even without exchanging too much personal information, it's interesting and you get a little window into a different life, so it's of benefit.

'As to whether it's sustainable to have thousands of "friends", well you'd have to put quite a bit of work in.

'Some people may feel a bit isolated or may not have a lot of genuine friends. For them, it may be a way of making up for not having friends in real life. Or perhaps they're just outgoing and extrovert, and it may just be their way of being able to have lots of superficial contact with lots of people.

'Real friendships need occasional face-to-face contact. But these days they are maintained somewhere between face-to-face contact and electronic contact – in the way that letters used to maintain friendship. College or university friendships are a good example. After they leave, people often wind up not seeing each other for years, then they get back in touch.

'Some of those friendships survive through a combination of Christmas cards, email and social networks, so networks are quite good in helping people keep in touch. Friendships can be maintained from a distance once they're established. I don't see why it should devalue the notion of friendship.'

MY STORY: 'WITH FRIENDS LIKE THESE...'

Holly Holmes, 24, Postgraduate Student

'My housemate in university put a thread up saying, 'Can everybody be back at six to clean the house'. This clearly didn't go down well (you always know when things don't go down well on Facebook because no one responds, even though you know everyone's seen it, because everyone's stuck in the library trying to revise, which inevitably means they've been on Facebook for the last two hours). Finally another housemate replied with, 'Well I think this is a bit cheeky, I've already cleaned the kitchen today...' and from then it was off. A full-blown row about the cleaning on Facebook. Stupid thing was, though, we never ever addressed it in real life. Not one person mentioned it. The whole house had been involved in this blazing row on a thread on Facebook, but you would have never know it. No one said a word.'

MY STORY: 'IF ANYONE ELSE EVER READ WHAT WE WROTE...'

Gareth Randall, 22, Teaching Assistant

'My friends and I have a running message feed going on Facebook. We've had it about three years now, God knows how long it would take you to read the whole thing. It's a feed that started because one of my friends posted a picture of someone we used to go to school with looking like an idiot. She made a little joke and it just went from there, we talk about everything and everyone on it. Mostly people we knew back in school – pictures of what they're doing now, who they're dating. It sounds awful of us, and really it is, but sometimes you look at who you went to school with and the awful pictures they put up of them out the night before and it's just too funny not to share. We always say though, if anyone ever read it, it would be terrible. Really terrible. It's basically a record of all the silly conversations we've had about other people. Plus links to their pictures to show our point. Basically the most incriminating thing ever – but also I bet every group of friends has one.'

MY STORY: 'DON'T BE HER FRIEND!'

Anna Walther, 26, Primary School Teacher

'Facebook can keep you in touch with your friends – AND your enemies. When I was in halls in university, there was an overseas student from Australia in our house. She was loud and daring and quite funny but there was also an element to her that made you aware you never wanted to get on the wrong side of her. One day all of us got a friend request from a girl we didn't know. She was from Australia, and her request came with a little personal message which went along the lines of "the girl you've made friends with is a b****, she stole my boyfriend off me when she didn't even care about him, she's done it before and she'll do it to one of you." Of course this caused uproar. The girl in our house swore the other girl had made the claims up, but we were never completely sure, and it just goes to show – you can go literally to the other side of the world and, through Facebook, your mistakes can follow you.'

MY STORY: 'HAVING A PARTY – AND YOU'RE NOT INVITED'

Dan Jacques, 23, Bar Attendant

'When we lived in our first student house there were seven of us – quite lot of people to keep happy at once. We got on great and it was a good year but, as with every other student house, there were inevitably times where we pissed each other off. I'm not talking serious incidents, though there were one or two that got pretty serious, but more like heated spats. One weekend one of my housemates created an event on Facebook for the weekend, trying to get all our friends out together. She called it "Cocktails and Camel" – Camel being this pretty cheesy, but pretty great RnB club in town. She invited all the housemates along – except me and one other. At first we were angry, but then we decided to create our very own event. We advertised it on Facebook as "PRIVATE FUNCTION", invited only ourselves and had the tagline as "the ONLY event worth attending tonight". We printed it off and stuck it on the fridge to make them feel extra guilty and then skipped out the door to get pissed in the pub. It totally worked because they came grovelling with tequila later!'

Defriending

If you can make friends online, you can also unmake them… Defriending – where you unceremoniously drop someone from your friends list – has become the scourge of modern social-networking life. You go to bed one night with 489 friends and wake up with 488. Who has dropped you? Why? Often you'll never find out, which just adds to the frustration.

In June 2010, in-house research carried out at Facebook showed that almost half of its 450 million users had 'defriended' someone. Many times this happens after the first flush of joining, when members try to connect with as many people as possible, has died down. In the cold light of day, they have misgivings about having added their workmates, or teachers, or granny and decide to quietly give them the cyber heave-ho. Often the other party will only find out they've been defriended when they are blocked from accessing someone's profile page, which can lead to feelings of real rejection, even if this was just a cyber-friendship.

The launch of Qwitter – a programme which lets you see who has stopped following you on Twitter and which tweet they might have objected to – demonstrates how sensitive an area it is. Facebook has its own defriender detective, an iPhone application that scrolls through your list of friends and lets you know if it has changed since the last time you logged on.

MOST COMMON REASONS FOR 'DEFRIENDING':

- Often narcissism and the need to project a certain image means many people use their updates to try to impress their 'friends' rather than just connect with them.
- Having hundreds of cyber-friends devalues real friendships.
- Social-networking is free of the constraints of time, geography and effort which have previously kept friendships naturally culled, so it means the friends that would normally have

dropped by the wayside, endure long after their sell-by date, retaining an access to your intimate life that you might no longer feel comfortable with, and creating a feeling of 'friend fatigue'.

The origins of 'defriending' are unclear, although we know that 30 January 2008 was unofficially declared, with the help of a Facebook group, International Delete Your MySpace Account Day, in what was an attempt to rally support for a mass defriending of one social-networking group by members of another. The fast-food giant, Burger King, capitalised on the trend with its 'Whopper Sacrifice' promotion. Facebook users who defriended 10 'friends' were rewarded with a coupon for a free burger. The campaign was so popular that people reportedly began to advertise on Craiglist for 'temporary friends'. 'Install Whopper Sacrifice on your Facebook profile, and we'll reward you with a free flame-broiled Whopper when you sacrifice ten of your friends,' went the blurb. To add to the indignity, the deleted friends would be sent a message and show up in the user's news feed, 'X sacrificed X for a free Whopper'.

In October 2010, Denver Business School from the University of Colorado, published the results of a survey analysing 1,500 Facebook accounts to find the top reasons for defriending. Fifty-seven per cent of those who'd removed someone from their friends' list had done so because of something that happened online, and 27 per cent because of something that happened in the real world. The top no-no's were:

1 Being Boring. Having to read what someone had for breakfast, or how big the traffic jam was on the way to work, isn't the best way of keeping online friends loyal.

2   Posting too often. When your news feed is dominated by just one friend updating all through the day, chances are you'll go for the 'delete' option.

3   Being too outspoken – particularly about politics and religion, or making racist or crude comments.

4   Using Facebook as a way of snooping on your children. Tempting, but a sure way to find yourself quietly dropped off the friends' list.

5   Splitting up. One day you're 'in a relationship', the next you're blocked from their profile. Harsh.

Coping with Cyber-Rejection

Being rejected hurts, whether it's face to face or through a computer network. Nobody wants to be rebuffed. Just as social-networking has brought with it a myriad of ways of connecting people, it's also brought just as many ways of disconnecting them – and none of them are much fun. In fact some people maintain that rejection via social media is actually more painful than in person because people are less likely to be diplomatic or sensitive when they're hiding behind a computer screen.

THE SOCIAL-NETWORKING REJECTION TOP 10

1   You send a friend request that never gets accepted.

2   You poke someone and they don't poke you back.

3   Joining a fast-moving thread that already has 20 witty comments, you add yours and immediately kill the thread stone dead.

4   You invite someone to a game of scrabble, and they never play their turn.

5 You get two comments on your birthday. And one of those is from your mum (the other is from you replying to the comment from your mum).

6 The number of people you're following is roughly 50 times the number of people following you. And you're following less than a 100 people.

7 You painstakingly tag all the people in the group shot with you – and one by one they de-tag themselves.

8 You start up a fan page – and nobody joins.

9 You invite friends to assess what kind of flower you are, or to think of an adjective that best describes you, starting with the third letter of their name, or to say which *Twilight* character you most resemble. And you get no responses (apart from your mum – again – who seems to think *Twilight* is some kind of natural history programme).

10 You start up another group – 'If this group gets 100,000 fans, I'm leaving Facebook' – and within 24 hours the membership is in six figures.

There's a tendency to think that social-networking is all light-hearted fun, but the fact is that even in cyberspace, it hurts to think that you're not liked, not appreciated or not wanted. Usually, it's not even meant as rejection, but without being able to see the other person or read the social context in which a remark was made or an action taken, it's impossible to tell how something was intended. Young people, who are just negotiating their way around the relationships minefield, are particularly vulnerable to the pain of rebuffal, whether imagined or otherwise.

5 WAYS TO HANDLE FACEBOOK REJECTION, BY PSYCHOLOGIST TAMMY MINDEL

1 Don't take it personally. The other person may have all sorts of different reasons for using Facebook; maybe you just don't suit their criteria. Maybe they want to limit themselves to 10 friends, perhaps they have a 'strictly professional' criteria for their use of Facebook. It could be one of many reasons why they're rejecting you. So don't instantly jump in with a negative, 'Oh I'm awful'. Stand back a bit and appreciate that it isn't about you at all.

2 Think positively about rejection. Look at it from the point of view of the advantages to you. For instance, it could be better for you not to be associated with that person. You could get a better result by contacting others who are more interesting – or you're more likely to have things in common with. By turning your thoughts around to a positive view, your emotional reaction to rejection becomes totally different. So focus on other, better, potential friends – who may have more to offer – and change your inner dialogue about yourself and your shortcomings.

3 Use the traditional methods of communication, if appropriate. If you already know the person and can't think why they'd reject you, because you already see yourself as friends, you always have the option to contact them by phone or meet up and talk it through in the normal way, rather than silently sulking or just leaving it up in the air. It could be a genuine mistake. Or there could be reasons you haven't thought of. Or know about. Talk it through – and clear the air.

4 Don't paint yourself into a corner with one rejection. Going onto Facebook is a risk – don't remove yourself completely by

vowing never to ask anyone to be your friend again. It might seem safer that way, never putting yourself up for rejection. But it isn't: all it means is you are denying yourself the opportunity of making other friends.

5 If you're a parent and your child is coping badly with a rejection, it's likely that they cope badly with it in the outside world, like at school. So as a parent, it's about trying to build your child's self-confidence. Try pointing out all the good, positive things about their personality, i.e. 'You've got lots of other nice friends' and 'Of course people appreciate you'. Build on the positive aspects of their existing social interaction; with a teenager, you could try explaining that to be confident individuals we all need to accept that rejection is part of taking risks in life.

PETWORKING

Not content with clogging up social-networking sites with superfluous friends, doting pet owners have also hijacked sites like Facebook, MySpace and Twitter to pass on news, updates and photos of their beloved animals, or increasingly to set up profile pages on their pet's behalf. Some have even gone further and created social-networking sites dedicated entirely to pets, where pampered pooches and mollycoddled moggies can build up networks of their best four-legged friends.

There are now hundreds of social 'petworking' sites to choose from, with users from all over the world. One of the biggest is Dogbook, an application from Facebook (www.apps.facebook.com/dogbook/). With two million users it expands by the day. Dogbook was such an immediate hit that it was soon followed by Catbook, Ferretbook, and

Rodentbook. Proud owners can post photos and videos of their pets, and share pet-keeping tips with other owners. Other petworking sites include Critterscorner.ning.com, Catster.com, Dogster.com and myDogspace.com and there's even one for rabbits: BunSpace.

Even pet charities have been getting in on the social-networking act, raising money through hosting events such as Twitter-based 'pawpawties' – online parties, often with a corporate sponsor – where animal-lovers pledge money for charities, which is then collected via other websites.

While most people see petworking as a harmless bit of fun, some safety and home-protection experts have warned that posting updates about your pet's daily habits, such as the time Barney likes to be walked and the particular route you take, could make owners a target for unscrupulous thieves.

Few advances in petworking have made pet-owners happier than the recent phenomenon of pet-posting where people create profiles and pose and post as their pets – even though, strictly speaking, creating a fake profile of any sort contravenes Facebook rules.

WHY MAKE A PROFILE PAGE FOR YOUR PET?

- Your family and friends might want to know that at 2.35pm, Fluffy played in his new pink hamster ball, and at 4.15pm, he was feeling a little bit sick but by 6.30, he was back on form and tucking into a sunflower seed snack.
- It's a way for you to show people what an offbeat, whacky sense of humour you have.
- If Mr Bubbles has all these lovely new Facebook friends to play with, surely it takes the pressure off you, as his owner, to entertain him?
- No need to think up constantly changing amusing, witty updates when your pet's life consists fundamentally of eat, poo, walk, sleep.

However, not everyone sees petworking as a harmless bit of fun. Some social commentators are concerned about the legal and moral implications of creating a false identity. 'It's a very simplistic way of demonstrating a false identity,' says social psychologist, Dr Arthur Cassidy. 'People who are not competent at describing themselves in a normal way, will use this animal symbolism. It's a way of using language to present a certain type of personality – warm or aggressive.

'For some people it's a way of compensating for their lack of words, but the worry is that creating a false identity and using animal icons could be a way to attract children. They will use any means possible to draw them in. Parents need to know how to spot this type of thing and teach children how to keep away from it.'

XX

For those of you who know my Mimi, she's having surgery today. The doctor says it doesn't look good but I'd really love for all of you to send positive thoughts and love her way. I think if the optimism and positivity radiates around her this will all go well. Pleas keep her in your thoughts today – she's way too important to my family to have anything happen to her.

YY

she's in my prayers

YY

Is this your dog? I can't even imagine losing my puppy :] I hope all goes well

XX

it's my grandma

Ask the Experts: Should Petworking Be Encouraged?

YES SAYS DR KAROL SZLICHINSKI, A PSYCHOLOGIST SPECIALISING IN NEW TECHNOLOGY

'By creating an online profile in the character of their cat or dog, people are saying that the pet is quite important in their life. And don't forget people do take on other people's voices quite often. Not all songs are autobiographical, for instance. Most novelists write successfully from different people's viewpoints.

'This can also bring humour too, i.e. "John's locked himself in his office and I can't have my usual walk today. I'll be lucky to get any food!"

'On the internet, you can be anyone you want to be. The usual reality checks are not always available, so you can indulge, in a good way, in a fantasy of a talking pet.'

NO, SAYS DR DAVID SMALLWOOD, ADDICTION COUNSELLOR AND PSYCHOTHERAPIST

Dr Smallwood believes that people who adopt their pet's persona to create an online world for it are frightened of revealing too much of themselves.

'They become a pet because it means they don't have to engage in any interaction or projection of their real selves at all and are living vicariously through their pet.'

In extreme cases, says Dr Smallwood, petworking could be a sign of deeper psychological issues:

'Let's just say you go out on the street and see someone walking up and down, talking to themselves quite loudly. How would you describe them? Mad? Becoming your pet online is a legitimate way of behaving like this.'

CELEBRITY PETWORKERS

When it comes to raising their pet's online profile, even the stars aren't averse to a bit of petworking...

1. Amy Winehouse

After her divorce from Blake Fielder-Civil, Amy remained in contact with her ex by sending him messages on Facebook via the Facebook page of her cat, Shirley. According to the *Sun* newspaper, Shirley, who proved remarkably articulate, sent touching comments to her former owner such as '*Oi mummy was saying to her friend about th time she made you breakfast an you drank all th nesquik til you was sick xxxxxxx.*' Sweet.

2. Courtney Love

In 2009 the unconventional singer delighted her followers by posting photos on her Twitter page of herself in bed with her pet turtle on her head.

3. Paris Hilton

The blonde heiress, known for coordinating her 13 dogs with her outfits, posted photos of her Mini Doggie Mansion on her Twitter page – an exact replica of her own luxurious Beverley Hills home, even down to the mini furniture. The two-storey building, overlooking the swimming pool in the grounds of Paris's home, featured a spiral staircase, a black chandelier, and wardrobes for the pooch's designer clothes as well as its own air-conditioning system. 'I have to admit, I may have spoiled them a little too much,' Paris tweeted on her Twitter page. 'But how can I not? Just look at those sweet lil' faces, they deserve to be treated like my lil' prince and princesses. I love my babies.'

4. 50 Cent

The controversial American rapper began tweeting as his miniature schnauzer, Oprah, in September 2010. OprahTheDog liked to post photos and tweet imaginary conversations with her superstar owner.

6

Celebrities

You'd think famous people might decide they have enough exposure without putting themselves on a social-networking site. Not a bit of it. While most of the profiles that appear on Facebook in the names of the great and the good are undoubtedly fakes, the stars do have a distinct online presence:

THE ROYALS

Many fake social-networking profiles have been set up purporting to be William Wales, or Her Maj, but some of the royals have actually joined the Facebook generation. Aside from an official British Monarchy Facebook page, Princes William and Harry both have pages on the site under secret names with very strict privacy settings. This follows the incident of the fake 'William Wales' who successfully added a number of Prince William's real friends who thought he was the real deal. Princesses Eugenie and Beatrice also have Facebook pages and have had to update their privacy settings after posting potentially embarrassing photos.

STEPHEN FRY

The celebrated wit and comedian single-handedly promoted the cause of Twitter back in February 2009 when he released a series of tweets while trapped in a lift for 40 minutes at London's Centre Point. 'Ok. This is now mad. I am stuck in a lift on the 26th floor of Centre Point. Hell's teeth. We could be here for hours. Arse, poo and widdle,' was his first tweet. Soon he was inundated with escape suggestions and time-killing advice from fellow Twitterers, all of which he shared with the others in the lift. 'Your brilliant comments are keeping us all hysterically cheerful,' he tweeted halfway through his ordeal. However, Fry has since come close to quitting his beloved Twitter on a couple of occasions – once after being called 'boring' by a follower, and again in protest at having been 'misquoted' in a newspaper interview where he supposedly suggested women didn't really like sex.

KANYE WEST

The American rapper made an unknown Coventry man into an overnight celebrity in the summer of 2010, by randomly picking him as the only person he would follow on Twitter. When Stephen Holmes tweeted to thank him for following him, West replied, 'You are the chosen one dun dun dun'. Holmes saw the number of people following him soar to 1,500 in the wake of the unexpected media attention. 'I feel pressure with my tweets now,' he admitted. 'Tweet strong young man tweet strong!!!' replied West. Sadly the Twitter relationship was not to last and just one week later, West withdrew his online support. 'Before this weekend I thought it would be cool to have a celebrity following me on Twitter,' Holmes told the *Coventry Telegraph* afterwards, 'but now I think it's really not worth it.'

West also voiced his gratitude to Twitter for providing an unbiased platform for him to tell his side of the MTV Video Music awards controversy where he grabbed the microphone from singer Taylor Swift and announced that his friend Beyoncé should have won. 'Man I love Twitter … I've always been at the mercy of the press but no more … The media tried to demonise me.'

John Mayer

Despite telling a CNN interviewer that quitting social-networking showed a failure of nerve – saying, 'You neuter your own Twitter account, you show fear. I think you show fear when you delete it.' – musician John Mayer quit microblogging in September 2010, leaving his 3.7 million Twitter followers disconsolate.

Simon Cowell

In contrast, this music mogul claimed to be distinctly under impressed by the whole social-networking phenomenon, reportedly saying in 2009, in response *American Idol* co-host Ryan Seacrest's apparent digs at his age on his Twitter page: 'Why would you want to talk to people like that? It's like phoning someone randomly whose number you don't even have and saying: "Hi, it's Simon, I went out with my family this weekend."'

We all love the way social-networking seems to have brought our favourite celebs within our orbit, making even the stars seemingly accessible. But celebrity networking is a two-way street, according to addiction counsellor Dr David Smallwood. 'The gain to the celebrity is publicity, marketing, exposure. The more candid you are on Twitter, the more likely you are to have fans follow what you say.

'But a lot of celebrities also feel that they NEED to do it. They need to be in that world because if they're not – they don't exist! It's all very contrived. It's there for a purpose – mostly so they can gain more publicity.'

Psychologist Dr Aric Sigman agrees that celebrities have been quick to recognise the potential of social-networking as a way of raising their public profile: 'They are looking for "presence" and a marketing tool in providing information for promotional purposes. It's a great way of letting people know what you are doing, what's coming up, when your next tour is – and perhaps correcting things written about you in the press.'

However, he warns that overexposure on social-networking sites could be counter-productive: 'One of the qualities of celebrity has always been a sense of mystique. By using Twitter or Facebook, they could be killing the mystique. That distance, that lack of presence made them terribly alluring once. Now they are falling over backwards to be in your face, just like a regular guy, just like you and I.

'Ultimately, the celebrities we really crave to know more about are those that seem somewhat aloof; we know just enough about them, what they do in their movies or their music; they shouldn't have to be chatting on social networks. They're famous, they play roles on the screen. Why lower themselves to mix with the rest of us?

'Celebrities using social-networking sites are bringing themselves down to an "off the shelf" level. A website with need-to-know information is fine but celebs don't need any of this social-networking they already have PR teams to tell the world what they're doing.'

Most Popular Celebrity Tweeters

At the end of 2009, mobile company INQ Mobile calculated the 'influence rating' of celebrity Twitter users worldwide, by measuring the number of times they tweeted, how good they were at re-tweeting other people's messages, and the number of times their posts were re-tweeted by other people. Their top five were:

1 Pete Cashmore, chief executive of Mashable, the highly
   influential social media blog.
2 P. Diddy.
3 Stephen Fry.
4 Oprah Winfrey.
5 Kim Karshadian.

The undisputed king and queen of celebrity twittering, of course, are Demi Moore and Ashton Kutcher. The couple constantly update their page, even posting photos of themselves flirting with each other by writing suggestive messages on their hands while in separate rooms. In 2009, Kutcher beat CNN in a race to be the first to amass one million Twitter followers (although his crown was soon snatched by Britney Spears).

However, according to scientists at Northwestern University, Illinois, who used specialised mathematical algorithms to rank the most influential people 'tweeting' on the hot topic of the day, having high numbers of followers doesn't correlate to having influence over people, or shaping 'trending' topics (issues popular at a given time). The conclusion was that people who were experts in their own field were more likely to be influential than high-profile celebrities.

TWEET HACKED

There was chaos in May 2010 when a Turkish hacker posted details of a loophole that allowed people to force celebrities to follow them on Twitter. Suddenly celebrities found themselves following thousands of complete strangers – who then had open access to their Twitter pages.

'Celebs now have to go in to their Twitter accounts and manually un-follow the hundreds of forced follows. TheDayTwitterExploded,' tweeted a put-out Perez Hilton.

Twitter sorted out that bug, but in doing so managed to temporarily erase follower lists, so that celebrities who'd amassed a large Twitter fan base now found themselves friendless – at least for the time it took to rectify the bug. Stephen Fry wrote: 'Do you know, I was sure I had more followers than that. Must have imagined it.'

MY STORY: 'WE TURNED OURSELVES INTO SHANIA TWAIN'

Ceara Elliot, 18, Student

'Me and my friends once did this hilarious thing where we created an account for Shania Twain. Now that in itself is funny but sort of something you forget in a week or so. I mean it was just part of a joke between us and we didn't really think anything of it. What was so good about this though was that, completely unsuspectingly, people believed it and we started getting added by loads of people, all with messages say how big of a fan they were, how much they "love your music" – it was crazy! In about a week we had about 600 friend requests. Of course we accepted all of them and just let all these fans gush over the wall about how much they loved Shania. It was only when one, obviously serious fan, wrote a really angry post saying that this must be a fake because we'd got her birthday wrong (it's not something we'd actually bothered to check of course) that people started deleting us. Still, to this day, Shania Twain still has over 700 friends and when her (fake) birthday rolls around (we stuck it at 28 August) she still gets a shedload of happy-birthday posts.'

CELEBRITY NARCISSISTS

Where Facebook has 'friends', Twitter has people you follow and people who follow you. It stands to reason that a well-balanced person would have more or less equal numbers of both, but some celebrities seem woefully weighted in one direction. In 2009, celebrity gossip website Holy Moly analysed stars' use of Twitter in a 'Celebrity Twitter Narcissism Rating' table to find which celebrities were the most self-obsessed. Russell Brand was identified as the biggest British narcissist, with 143,548 followers compared to only 14 that he himself was following (one of whom was Jonathan Ross, and another David Baddiel). Lily Allen wasn't far behind, notching up 101,500 followers but tracking just ten people including fellow pop star Britney Spears, model Alexa Chung and comic Alan Carr. In third place was Radio One DJ Chris Moyle, with 106,013 followers and following just 13 people. Stephen Fry, on the other hand, was found to be one of the more generous celebrities, following 55,251 people at the time.

Celebrity Tweet Wars

LORD ALAN SUGAR VS. KIRSTY ALLSOP
There were no prisoners taken in the spat between Lord Sugar and property princess Kirsty Allsop. Ms Allsop dubbed the Amstrad tycoon 'shockingly uncharitable', while Lord Sugar hit back, calling her the 'worst celeb ever in celeb *Apprentice*'.

KELLY OSBOURNE VS. DANNII MINOGUE
When Dannii complained in her 2010 autobiography about the reportedly bullying behaviour of fellow *X Factor* judge Sharon Osbourne, Osbourne's daughter Kelly leapt to her mum's defence on Twitter. 'The best thing to happen to Dannii was my mother hated her she needs to shut her mouth and concenterate [sic] on motherhood!' Kelly tweeted. She went on to add: 'to the 12 dannii fans out there i ask you this question what would you do if someone wrote a book of lies about your mother?' Later, her tweets got even more impassioned: 'sorry i have just had to deal with this bulls—t 4 years and i have kept my mouth shut but i am sick of her lies enough is enough'

GILLIAN MCKEITH VS. BEN GOLDACRE
@GillianMcKeith, believed to be the Twitter account for celebrity nutritionist Gillian McKeith (aka 'Poo Lady'), was incensed when in July 2010 an unknown Twitterer posted about reading Ben Goldacre's book, *Bad Science*, which calls into question McKeith's

academic qualifications. In a series of angry tweets McKeith branded Goldacre an 'ass', his book 'lies', and attacked the user for 'anti-American bigotry'. These tweets were quickly deleted but not before Goldacre had responded informing McKeith that he considered her allegation about his book libellous. After tweeting-and-deleting that her detractors were 'chavs', a series of tweets appeared in McKeith's feed outlining her qualifications from a third person perspective. These, too, were quickly deleted. Things then got even weirder when McKeith appeared to deny that she was the real Gillian McKeith, despite the account apparently being linked directly from her official website.

LILY ALLEN VS COURTNEY LOVE

When Lily Allen posted an unflattering picture of Courtney Love on Twitter in March 2010, calling her a 'drug addled lunatic' via the site, the former Mrs Kurt Cobain didn't let it lie.

'That's just baby brat nonsense. Wouldn't deign to post a picture of her thighs,' she tweeted, before turning the drug abuse allegations back on Allen herself. In later tweets, Lily seemed to have taken a more conciliatory stance. 'Sorry that was mean. Enuff of these juvenile musings, I should never have risen to the bait. Silly Lily.'

AMY WINEHOUSE VS. MARK RONSON

Never famous for keeping a low public profile, in September 2010, singer Amy Winehouse apparently used her Twitter page to accuse old friend and *Back to Black* producer, Mark Ronson, of taking too much credit for the famous record. She tweeted: 'Ronson, you're dead to me. One album I write and you take half the credit – make a career out of it? Don't think so BRUV.' Within days she seemed to be having second thoughts. 'Ronson I love you; that make it better? You know I love you,' came her follow-up olive-branch tweet.

DENISE VAN OUTEN VS. NATALIE CASSIDY

When Denise Van Outen saw Natalie Cassidy with her six-week-old baby on Lorraine Kelly's morning programme in November 2010, promoting her new reality TV show just a few months after Cassidy had publicly criticised Van Outen for going back to work soon after giving birth, she was outraged at what she felt was Cassidy's hypocrisy – and expressed her feelings on Twitter.

FACEBOOK CELEBRITY DOPPELGANGER WEEK

February 2010 saw an unofficial launch of 'Celebrity Doppelganger Week' on Facebook, with users all over the world encouraged to swap their profile picture for portraits of famous people they think they look like. For those struggling, MyHeritage created a page that helped users find their Doppelganger celeb.

LADY GAGA: WORLD'S MOST POPULAR CELEBRITY SOCIAL NETWORKER

According to Twitaholic.com, which publishes a list of the top 100 celebrity Twitaholics based on followers, Lady Gaga took over the first place spot from Britney Spears in late summer 2010. She had already overtaken Barack Obama to become the most popular living person on Facebook, with nearly over 19million Facebook friends. Famecount, which analyses the most popular celebrities, sports teams and movies across the whole social-networking spectrum, rates Lady Gaga as the most popular person online when adding up her Facebook, Twitter and YouTube statistics.

'Yes, your profile picture is fine. Is that all ?'

7
Stalking

The great thing about social-networking is that it means lots of people can be kept up to date with what's going on in your life. The scary thing about social-networking is… that it means lots of people can be kept up to date with what's going on in your life.

> **XX**   Status Update
>
> find myself coming to your profile page a lot today. Perhaps it is because of that uber sexy hair!! I somewhat want to play with it.
>
> **YY**
>
> Errr… That's a bit weird, XX.
>
> **XX**
>
> I won't apologise for the truth

The golden age of social-networking has brought with it the golden age of online stalking. Never has it been easier to contact and track the object of your affections – or disaffections – whichever the case might be.

Bitter or lovesick exes are the most common culprits, often torturing themselves by compulsively logging into their former beloved's profile online, keeping abreast of what they're doing and who they're seeing, either directly or through mutual friends in the same network.

YOU KNOW YOU'RE A FACEBOOK STALKER WHEN...

- Your heart stops every time you see one of those 'see who has been viewing your profile' fake applications.
- You find yourself scrolling through photo albums of people you don't even know, just because a certain person was tagged in one of them.
- You've been caught out asking 'how was the party/film/lunch with your parents', before realising the only way you could know about that was by reading his or her wall posts to other people.
- You've checked out every one of his or her friends' profiles – all 736 of them.
- You know the second anyone buys him or her a Sex on the Beach, or tends their crops or superpokes them – *and you don't like it.*

MY STORY: 'HIS FACEBOOK SPYING FREAKED HER OUT'

Hester Allaway, 23, Student

'A friend of a friend of mine once met this girl in a bar. They got talking and he bought her a few drinks and he asked if he could see her again. She said yeah sure and gave him her number. All pretty standard stuff. Anyway, when he got home he searched for her on Facebook. Her profile happened to be fairly open so he had a look round her profile, as you do, and texted her later that week asking her if she'd like to go out for a drink. She said she'd love to and they arranged a time and a place that weekend. Before the big date he had one last look round her Facebook. He noted her favourite song was 'Lady in Red' so when he picked her up in the car he made sure it was playing as she got in. They had dinner, had a couple of drinks and he drove her home. She asked if he'd like to come in. He went inside. One thing led to another and they went to bed. As things hotted up, he couldn't help himself, he burst into song, singing – you've guessed it – 'Lady in Red'. After that, not unsurprisingly, he never heard from her again. But it seems worth it from the enjoyment he gets telling the story in the pub.'

MY STORY: 'BE MY FRIEND – SO I CAN SPY ON YOU FOR MY SISTER'

Harriet Hobson, 20, PA

'I once got added by this guy on Facebook. I thought it was someone else so I accepted and didn't think much of it but a few days later he popped up on my feed and I realised I didn't know who he was at all. I messaged him after a little while and asked exactly where we knew each other from. He took a few days to message me back but finally came this reply: '*You didn't hear it from me but my sister told me to add you. Her friend is madly in love with your boyfriend and is desperate to get in with a chance. They asked me to add you so they could get into your Facebook and spy on you properly.*' It was kind of funny really. I mean, it's soooo annoying when you want to spy on someone but you can only see their profile picture, but I never thought someone would be trying to do that to me!'

DOES FACEBOOK FACILITATE OBSESSIVE LOVE? THE EXPERTS SPEAK:

'It's much easier to be infatuated with someone on social-networking sites,' says Dr David Smallwood, independent addiction counsellor. 'In fact they act as a catalyst for making it obsessive – because you won't get rejected. If someone is susceptible to this kind of infatuation or obsessiveness, Facebook facilitates it.'

Social psychologist Dr Arthur Cassidy agrees that there's a danger of social-networking providing a platform for people to indulge in obsessive behaviour. 'People use social-networking to create false identities with which to meet new people. This type of relationship can become obsessive because it's something you're not exposed to in real life – it's new, fascinating, it can satisfy some of your desires. So if you're not satisfied with your current relationship, you're more likely to find some kind of satisfaction by getting involved with social-networking. There's intrigue involved. Every day presents a situation where you could meet someone new. And that is stimulating. We're driven a lot by novelty, our behaviour is stimulated 24 hours a day by our reactions to things. Social-networking is a novelty. You don't know what is coming next.

'That becomes a high motivator to keep looking at it, again and again. You are hoping that every time you turn on that computer, there will be someone who will satisfy all your motivations and desires.

'Every human being has 16 basic motives, we turn them on and off every day. That is why people become obsessive about social-networking or even addicted – it turns the different motives on and off all the time.

'Suppose a guy is bad at selecting women. His motivation for attraction means he keeps getting it wrong. Yet on Facebook he can create a new identity, a false persona. We always exaggerate ourselves, everyone does.'

Social-networking Stalkers in the News

- In April 2010, *BBC Crimewatch* presenter Rav Wilding, won his case against Toneeta Beckford who was found guilty of harassing him via Facebook and Twitter. Toneeta Beckford sent 'vile and grotesque' abuse over the social-networking sites and threatened that she would 'see him on Judgement Day' and hoped he broke a leg while taking part in *Strictly Come Dancing*. Even after Wilding blocked her from his Facebook and Twitter sites, he continued to receive messages from her under different names. Later Beckford used her own Facebook page to describe the messages as 'a joke'.

- When IT worker Paul Bristol, saw photos on Facebook of his ex-girlfriend with another man, he flew back from Trinidad to Britain, where he stabbed Camille Mathurasingh repeatedly in her home in Bromley-by-Bow, East London. Bristol then stabbed himself in a failed suicide attempt and in March 2010, he was jailed for a minimum of 22 years.

- In December 2009, Jacques More became one of the first people in the UK to be jailed for stalking someone on Facebook. He breached a restraining order, claiming that the subject of his attentions had contacted him first – spiritually.

- Jason Smith was given a lifetime restraining order in March 2009 after bombarding Alexandra Scarlett's Facebook and MySpace accounts with threatening messages. For two years, Scarlett repeatedly shut down her accounts and opened new ones, but he always tracked her down. She also tried blocking his Facebook page, but he set up new ones on which he would post intimidating messages for her.

MY STORY: 'SOMEONE STOLE MY IDENTITY'

Ellie Kemp, 21, Student

'In the early days of Facebook, before all the privacy settings were tightened up, I had the strangest experience. I was typing in celebrity names to see if I could find famous Facebook or MySpace users. I started searching for the *Skins* cast, and a MySpace account popped up under the name of the actor who played Cassie. I opened it up, and to my horror found it was an account with all my profile pictures on it! Somebody had found my Facebook page, and stolen all my pictures – it was the weirdest experience. There was even one with me and my brother which had been captioned something like "me and my boyfriend on holiday". I couldn't believe it. The more I saw of the page, the more I kept thinking how weird this all was. This person had taken my pictures, and somebody else's name, and created a person who didn't exist. After I bombarded the account with messages, I eventually got one back from the girl who'd made the page saying she was sorry, it was a project for work. It really was so strange. Anyway she took the page down once she knew I'd found it, but I will always remember first seeing my own face as somebody else's profile.

MY STORY: 'I TURNED INTO A FACEBOOK STALKER'

Sam Taylor, 21, Unemployed

'Me and my girlfriend went on holiday to America a couple of summers ago, really nice, away for two months, travelling down the West Coast and stopping at cities along the way. Seeing as we were doing the West Coast, we decided to start in Vancouver because it was just next to America on the Canadian boarder and my parents had been and said it was nice. Vancouver was lovely, and we spent quite a lot of time in a bar down the road from our hostel called "Chill Winston". Partly because it was on the way into town and the White

Russians were really good but mostly because I fell head over heels in love with the waitress. Now I wasn't actually in love with this girl of course, but she was just so nice and pretty, I didn't mind dragging my girlfriend in every night before we went out to have a quick cocktail and gaze at her from our seats. A few months later I remembered this girl on a lazy hungover Sunday in front of the TV. I got my laptop and searched Chill Winston on Facebook to see if I could find her on the group. There were plenty of members but I couldn't see any of them because they were all in different networks. I figured the only way round this was to create a new Facebook account, join the Vancouver network and browse though the members of the group. This I did and I was just absent-mindedly flicking through when I looked at the clock. I suddenly realised I'd spent five hours searching for a girl who lived in Canada whose name I didn't even know. I'd created a new profile, searched through social groups in Canada, added people I didn't know. I couldn't believe it, I hadn't even really been thinking about it, I'd just sat there on Facebook for hours on end. I was appalled with myself! What was I doing? And to make it worse – I never did find the girl.'

MY STORY: 'IS IT JUST ME, OR IS THIS KIND OF CREEPY...?'

Dora Mortimer, 22, Administrator

'When I dislocated my knee last winter I was weeks away from going on holiday to Berlin for the weekend to visit a friend who was living there for the year. Dislocating my knee was bad enough, but the thought of getting on a plane, going to a foreign country during their freezing winter, and battling snow on crutches just seemed like it would be ridiculous. Still – it was all booked and there was a bunch of us going so I thought, why not? I'm sure it will be fine. It was, sort of fine, but mostly because it only seemed sensible that I hire a wheelchair rather than struggle through the snow. On the way back two German airport staff helped me onto the plane, which was a bit of a struggle on the freezing cold runway and with a huge bulky wheelchair. I felt really bad for them and was nice as possible when saying thank you. When I got home that evening I checked Facebook and one of the German airport staff had sent me a message saying that he hoped I got home safe! It was quite weird, I guess he would have had to look at my passport and memorise the name to have found me. Although, I guess, it's quite creepy, I think he was probably just being nice – but it is strange how Facebook allows complete strangers to get in touch...'

MY STORY: 'I ADMIT IT, I'M A FACEBOOK SNOOPER'

Maura Nielson, 24, Retail Assistant

'If you happen to find yourself in a bored and evil mood I would recommend a little recreational time snooping round the cyber skeletons lurking on everyone's Facebook profile. A game I like to play, one that has successfully whiled away many hours pretending to do Uni work, is to pick a friend on Facebook, preferably someone you've only known for a couple of years, and click on their photos but instead of pressing "next" press "previous" i.e. the first photo ever uploaded of them. I'm not proud of myself for admitting this particular pastime but it's great for unearthing a dodgy hairdo or a well-hidden chubby period; also you get the added bonus of flicking from first photo to most recent, thus producing a kind of "before" and "after" effect.'

Cyber-stalked Celebrities

Social-networking has also been a gift to obsessive fans who can now get access to a celebrity or public figure in ways that never would have been possible before.

1. Brian McFadden and Delta Goodrem

The ex-Westlife star and his girlfriend were subjected to a torrent of abuse on Twitter by a cyber-stalker, calling himself 'Saviour Mankind' who declared his love for Goodrem and threatened McFadden should he ever 'harm a hair on Delta's head'.

2. KIM KARDASHIAN

The reality TV star claimed to be 'extremely frightened', after a man who had stalked her in 'real life' sometimes made up like the Joker from *Batman*, went on to violate a restraining order by renewing contact via Twitter in August 2010.

3. KERRY KATONA

The former Atomic Kitten singer contacted police after a woman she had accepted as a Facebook friend allegedly turned up at her home in Cheshire. Katona was reportedly given advice by Merseyside Police about personal security and privacy while on social-networking sites.

STALKING APPLICATION?
In September 2010, it became known that Facebook was testing a new feature called 'subscribe to', which would enable users to subscribe to another user's Facebook profile so that they would be automatically updated every time that person posts something or uses any of the other Facebook activities.

Just in case Facebook and Twitter weren't giving stalkers enough of a forum to exercise their stalking tendencies, a new social network was launched in August 2010 – TopStalker.com – which encourages anyone spotting someone famous out and about to snap a photo and upload it onto the site for others to comment on.

In October 2010, Twitter cut its links with website JustSpotted.com amid fears that it could encourage the stalking of celebrities. The website, which was developed in conjunction with several social-networking sites aimed to use celebrity postings on social-networking sites and public sightings to collate information about stars and their whereabouts, which could then be used to track them on a world map. However, Twitter withdrew its support amid concerns the site could violate celebrities' privacy.

8

Politics

Canny politicians caught on early to the potential of networking sites to raise their public profiles – particularly when it came to young voters. Obviously they want to get their message across and win votes, but networking sites are also seen as important in winning over a disaffected younger generation to a party political process that many feel is not relevant to them.

Recently there has been a trend away from the individual web pages and blogs of the early Noughties, with politicians' energies moving onto networking sites. By the beginning of 2010 more politicians were tweeting than blogging.

The master politician of social-networking is President Obama. His 2008 presidential campaign was generally agreed to have made the best use yet of networking sites and set the bar high. He used Facebook, Twitter, YouTube and other sites to campaign, to mobilise grass-roots support, and also to fundraise with micro-donations from ordinary people. And of course it all paid off.

After he won, Obama tweeted: 'We just made history. All of this happened because you gave your time, talent and passion. All of this happened because of you. Thanks.' Strange then that in a 2009 speech he claimed: 'I have never used Twitter'. Oh the joy of a large staff...

2010 UK General Election

In the 2010 UK general election campaign, all parties tried to learn from Obama's campaign by making use of the main networking sites, with varying degrees of success.

2010 ELECTION SOCIAL-NETWORKING SUCCESS STORIES:

- The Conservatives encouraged their supporters to launch their own successful Facebook page as Obama had.
- Labour's Members net page followed Obama's example in successfully mobilising 'feet on the ground'.
- In the 2010 UK General Election, Facebook and YouTube hosted the first online debate, with users submitting questions for the three party leaders.

However, not all their attempts were successful. As the campaign mounted, politicians were roundly lampooned.

2010 UK ELECTION SOCIAL-NETWORKING FAILURES:

- Gordon Brown's foray onto YouTube, talking about the expenses scandal, was roundly mocked.
- David Cameron's campaign poster, 'We can't go on like this. I'll

cut the deficit not the NHS' was twisted and tweeted with a pic of Cameron with a quiff saying 'We can't go on like this, with suspicious minds'.

- A spoof video on YouTube of Cameron singing an adapted version of Pulp's 'common people', which included the immortal line 'And then I'll s**t on common people like you', got 750,000 hits.

- Before the election, David Cameron reportedly ordered all Conservative politicians to have all tweets and Facebook entries approved by the party. Perhaps he has a point – research by TweetGuv found that three-in-ten tweets by politicians were not in line with party policy.

- Cameron is said to be doubtful about Twitter and apologised after saying on the radio 'Too many tweets might make a tw*t'.

Not everyone sees the marriage of social-networking and politics as one made in heaven. Some argue that reducing complex policy messages to soundbites undermines proper debate. 'Politicians using Facebook and Twitter are truly hurting the electorate with their simplified ways of presenting things. A newsflash for all those new grassroots movements starting up about now: politics are complicated. Invest a good amount of time in researching what people believe before you throw your undying support behind them,' says online journalist Ryan MacNair.

A survey tracking online conversations during the UK 2010 election found more negative than positive sentiment for each party leader.

But there are signs that social-networking sites may be less effective publicity tools than politicians like to think. A 2010 Hansard Society audit reported that only four per cent of people use Facebook to follow political parties. Two per cent follow on Twitter. Newspapers and TV claim that they still set the agenda.

President Obama

President Obama's Facebook page has more than 15million followers. Nonetheless Duane Raymond of Fairsay.com reports that Joe Rospers, the Obama Campaign Online Director, told him, 'The value of supporters on social-networking sites was in the "single digits", so fewer than 10 per cent of support originated from the social-networking sites. While they had a lot of membership and publicity around their social-networking support, it produced little tangible results in terms of donations or participation. It likely helped recruit some supporters and supported the impression of a youthful and trendy campaign.'

THE SECRETS OF OBAMA'S LEGENDARY CAMPAIGN

- Obama realised that YouTube meant that his speeches could be widely seen in full, rather than as soundbites on TV news.
- He maintained interest with active, regular blogging.
- My.Barackobama.com is a ground-breaking interactive supporters site, where users can set up their own page, join groups and get involved.

Political Activism

It's not only the big guns of politics that have recognised the potential of social-networking sites. At a grassroots level, activists from all walks of life have also discovered the power of networking to promote charitable causes, social activism and grassroots political causes.

HAITI

In the early hours following the 2010 Haiti earthquake, the power of networking sites to disseminate information and act as a hub for action was shown at its best – they were crucial in transmitting information within the country and to the outside world. Some of the first images of the devastation were uploaded onto YouTube and other sites. Networking sites were also used by Haitians and aid workers for communication within the country after the earthquake, and played a part in fund raising.

Most charities have pages on the main social-networking sites, and separate pages for particular campaigns. This quote from the campaign central website comes from Kate Allen of Amnesty International UK:

'We won't ever stop protesting on the streets and outside embassies. But now social networks are where people are coming together to get fired up about issues and take action. The Unsubscribe campaign puts social media at the heart of human rights campaigning, bringing people together online and making our voice louder than ever. Online and on the streets, in social media and traditional media, Unsubscribe will engage with people who passionately believe in the right to a fair trial and the right not to be tortured.'

Sites like Meetup.com, which started out as a kind of dating site and evolved into a huge network of local groups, have attracted non-profit, community and campaigning organisations wanting to garner support, spread the message and publicise events.

Some media-savvy charities have even started their own social-networking sites. Macmillan Cancer Support started out hosting forums and these have developed into a successful networking site for cancer sufferers, whatnow.org.uk.

Social-networking sites claim huge success rates in mobilising popular support for grassroots political action and for enabling communication from countries where the media is controlled. When thousands of Moldavians organised a joint action in 2009 via networking sites, and gathered to protest against their government, their protest was dubbed the Twitter revolution. Twitter was credited with keeping communications open and allowing cohesion in a fast-changing situation.

Similarly, Facebook, Flickr, YouTube, Twitter and Mashups were all used extensively in the Kenyan election in 2006, for information sharing and mobilisation, as the mainstream media was restricted.

But it is probably in Iran more than anywhere else that networking sites have come to be seen as crucial to political action. A campaign page on Facebook is calling for Twitter to be nominated for a Nobel Peace Prize, for its role facilitating anti-government activists in Iran. During the post-2009 election protest, Twitter was logging 220,000 tweets per hour about that part of the world.

'When traditional journalists were forced to leave the country, Twitter became a window for the world to view hope, heroism, and horror. It became the assignment desk, the reporter, and the producer. And, because of this, Twitter and its creators are worthy of being considered for the Nobel Peace Prize,' writes Mark Pfeifle, a former American national security adviser, on the site. YouTube was also seen as crucial in Iran. As the government tried to limit contact with the outside world and contain protests, scores of amateur video of violence and incidents were posted.

BUT DOES IT REALLY WORK?

Not everyone is convinced about the power of social-networking sites to facilitate real change. Malcolm Gladwell, the best-selling author and thinker, argued in the New Yorker magazine in October 2010 that sites like Facebook promote 'weak ties' that encourage shows of support, but not real –potentially dangerous – activism.

Most of our friends on social-networking sites are likely to be acquaintances we have never met, not close friends or family – and it is only these sort of intimate ties that move us to real action, he argues. So it is easy to get numbers for an online campaign, but that doesn't translate into action or generous giving.

'The Facebook page of the Save Darfur Coalition has 1,282,339 members, who have donated an average of nine cents apiece,' Gladwell points out.

'Facebook activism succeeds not by motivating people to make a real sacrifice but by motivating them to do the things that people do when they are not motivated enough to make a real sacrifice,' he concludes.

SOCIAL-NETWORKING AS A CAMPAIGNING TOOL

- Social-networking sites provide free access to a massive audience of potential supporters. They also have the benefit that as your group or campaign builds, supporters can contribute material easily.
- However, networking sites are not tailor-made for campaigns – you will for example get lots of post you don't want on your wall, and it will require maintenance.
- Before you do anything, work out what you are trying to achieve. Unfocused promotion on a networking site will leave supporters frustrated, and they will wander off. Be specific. Are you looking for funding? Or to raise awareness of an issue? Or for support? A clearly focused message is your starting point.
- For detailed instructions and lots of tips on setting up a site with a political aim, download digiactive's guides to Facebook Activitism and Twitter Activism.

IN THE PAPERS: A THOROUGHLY MODERN PROTEST

The student protests in November 2010, which began as a peaceful demonstration against increases in university fees but ended in a riot with protesters storming the Conservative Party HQ, Millbank Tower in Westminster, were massively influenced by social media. The protests were largely co-ordinated by groups and pages on Facebook, while Twitter was used by protesters in particular locations to keep track of what was going on elsewhere. The police proved themselves equally technologically savvy when they used Twitter to communicate with rioters on the roof of Millbank Tower.

'She's just done her first tweet.'

9

Living through Tweeting

For most people, social-networking is something we do in our spare time, a leisure activity. But as we saw with the groom who tweeted at the altar, there are some people who see social-networking as intrinsic to their everyday life and who believe no subject should be off-limits for Facebook friends or Twitter followers.

When Penelope Trunk, a 42-year-old American who runs a social-networking site for managing careers and a popular blog, tweeted in September 2009 that she was having a miscarriage at work, there was an instant furore. Television and newspapers around the world fell over themselves to declare their outrage and claim that a line had been crossed. Some things were just too intimate to be revealed on a social-networking site, was the general consensus.

However, Trunk disagreed. 'I have tweeted about my sex life, my period, and even a minor run-in with the police. For me, Twitter is a way to make a note about the most important things that happen in the day,' she wrote in the *Guardian* in November 2009, going on to argue that miscarriage is a part of a woman's experience and therefore shouldn't be deemed taboo. Trunk also claimed that only 70 of the people who subscribe to her Twitter feed had unsubscribed, indicating that those for whom the tweet was intended were not those who found it offensive.

For many people updating on social-networking sites has become almost as natural as breathing, to the extent that something can't actually be happening if they haven't seen it on Facebook or Twitter. That's why so many of us even insist on updating while on holiday, unable to relax unless we've filled our online friends in about our every movement.

A survey published in May 2009 by lastminute.com revealed that 42 per cent of people in the 18 – 24 age group now admit to spending time off updating online pages or microblogs rather than seeing the sights.

In August 2010, Liz Hurley raised a few (perfectly plucked) eyebrows with her frequent tweeting while on holiday with her husband and son in sun-drenched St Tropez. The actress updated her followers on everything from the books she was reading to where she'd had lunch and even what everyone had had for breakfast.

Even more worrying than networking while on holiday is the trend towards updating while behind the wheel. In October 2010, an RAC report revealed that more than one in five motorists (21 per cent) admitted they were likely to check a social media site or surf the net while driving. The most popular activities are emailing (11 per cent), checking Google Maps (9 per cent), downloading music

(9 per cent), checking photos (8 per cent) and visiting Facebook (7 per cent).

Things are no better on the other side of the Atlantic, where a 2009 report by online measurement service Crowd Science, found that one-in-ten twitterers admitted posting to the social network while driving at least once during the 30 days before being questioned. Crowd Science said the Twitter result compared to about five per cent of other social media users who confessed to posting while driving. The same study revealed that 17 per cent of Twitter users confessed to accessing the site from the loo, while nearly a third (31 per cent) say they tweet from restaurants. Twice as many twitterers as non-twitterers also owned up to accessing the site during a play or live performance.

There's no place off-limits it seems, not even the Wimbledon changing rooms, where stars like Andy Murray and Serena Williams regularly update their followers on events on and off court. In May 2009, history was made when astronaut Mike Massimino made the first ever tweet from space, although he has since been joined by several others, including Japanese astronaut Soichi Noguchi, who used the social-networking site to send hundreds of photos of earth and space taken from the Space Shuttle Atlantis and the International Space Station.

IN THE PAPERS: I GAVE BIRTH ON TWITTER!

Most women in labour find it hard to remember their own names let alone go online, but in September 2010 nursery nurse Fi Star-Stone tweeted her way through a 13-hour home birth, hoping to help 'dispel the myths of childbirth'. The Stafford woman, who already had a daughter, even posted nine tweets from her iPhone while in a birthing pool, earning her hundreds of new fans and followers.

Social-networking Group

The idea of social media isn't just that it puts you in touch with people you already know, but also that you connect with strangers who happen to share the same interests. To that end, sites like Facebook abound with groups, pages and causes which users can sign up to and 'meet' other like-minded folk, even if it is only in cyberspace.

In February 2010, the number of Facebook groups was put at 620 million, and that's not including the millions of Facebook pages, initially intended as marketing tools for brands or public figures to collect 'fans', but now often interchangeable with groups.

According to Facebook's own figures, there are more than 900 million 'objects' (pages, groups, events and community pages) that users interact with.

Twitter, not to be outdone, has lists, based on bringing together users who share similar interests, industries and friends, although as yet they don't seem to attract the same following in terms of sheer numbers as the most popular Facebook pages and groups.

It seems few of us can resist the allure of feeling like we belong to something bigger than ourselves. But what is the psychology behind these often phenomenally successful online presences?

- **Identity** – By signing up to groups or fan-pages or lists, we are helping other people define us as well as clarifying our own sense of identity.

- **Community** – Humans need to feel connected to those around them and to feel some kind of measure of mutual support, even if it is only of the cyber variety.

- **Solidarity** – The need to stand shoulder-to-shoulder with other people against some common enemy or in favour of a common cause, is fundamental for many people.

- **Social Interaction** – Online groups offer the chance to interact with other people, most of whom we won't know, with the safety net of being 'remote', so that you're not taking the same social and psychological risks as if these were face-to-face interactions. This is very empowering for people who might find normal social situations difficult, but who still yearn for some kind of meaningful interaction with others.

- **Intimacy** – By owning up to the things that are important to us, or that we find amusing or outrageous or unfair, we are inviting a degree of intimacy with others and admitting where the sensitive points in our defences lie.

- **Self-expression** – Everyone wants to be heard. Social-networking groups are an easy, accessible way of expressing our opinions, often to a much wider audience than we would normally reach. And because of the specialised nature of the group, we can be reasonably sure that audience will be receptive to our views.

- **Social Conscience** – Getting involved in causes and groups outside of those that relate specifically to our own interests, is deemed by psychologists to lead to a higher degree of personal fulfilment.

Some Infamous Social-networking Campaigns:

CAT IN A WHEELIE BIN

After an outraged cat-owner posted CCTV footage on YouTube in August 2010 of a woman passer-by casually dropping their pet into a wheelie bin, there began a Facebook campaign to name and shame the culprit. Tens of thousands of people signed up to the group designed to identify the middle-aged woman, who was finally unmasked as 45-year-old Mary Bale, a former bank worker from Coventry. In October 2010, Bale admitted to causing the animal 'unnecessary suffering' and was fined £250, ordered to pay £1,171 in costs and banned from keeping animals for five years. A Facebook page which advocated death to Mary Bale and attracted thousands of fans, was later taken down by site moderators.

JUSTICE FOR RAOUL MOAT

Killer Raoul Moat, who shot dead one man and left two other people seriously injured, and died after evading police capture for several days, was misguidedly romanticised by a vocal minority who insisted on seeing him as a modern-day Robin Hood figure. His supporters rallied around a Facebook tribute page created by Siobhan O'Dowd, called 'R.I.P. RAOUL MOAT YOU LEGEND!' At one stage the group had nearly 40,000 fans, moving Prime Minister David Cameron to express his deep concern about the existence of the group and several public figures to urge Facebook to remove it. 'It is absolutely clear that Raoul Moat was a callous murderer, full stop, end of story,' said the PM. 'I cannot understand any wave, however small, of public sympathy for this man. There should be sympathy for his victims and the havoc he wreaked in that community. There should be no sympathy for him.' The social-networking giant refused to budge on its position, citing freedom of speech as its overriding motivation. However, the group's creator herself eventually withdrew the page, saying she was worried about her own safety after receiving death threats.

BOOBQUAKE

In April 2010, a young American science blogger called Jennifer McCreight responded to a statement by Iranian cleric Hojatoleslam Kazem Sedighi that women who dress immodestly have brought about an increase in the incidence of earthquakes, by suggesting that on a certain day, 26 April 2010, women should dress deliberately wantonly in order to test his claims. She dubbed the project 'Boobquake'. She originally assumed that only friends and blog-readers would be involved, but the idea soon went viral, with word being spread largely through social-networking sites such as Facebook and Twitter, which helped recruit around one hundred thousand women to the cause. 'I encourage other female sceptics to join me and embrace the supposed supernatural power of their breasts,' McCreight said on the Boobquake Facebook page. 'Or short shorts, if that's your preferred form of immodesty.'

In the event, even an earthquake in Taiwan, measuring 6.5 on the Richter scale, wasn't enough to convince McCreight and her skimpily dressed followers that there was any truth in the Iranian cleric's claims. 'Even though Boobquake wasn't perfect, it still was a success,' McCreight wrote in the *Guardian*. 'The vast majority of people – including earthquake researchers, feminists, and many Iranians – thanked me for this exercise in scepticism.'

Using Social-networking Groups to Affect Change

Seeing how political groups and charities were harnessing the power of social-networking to push for change, popular culture wasn't about to be left behind.

Agitating via social media is fast becoming the weapon of choice for anyone wanting to argue against a football manager's choice of players, or a particular person to be voted in or out of *X Factor*. Some examples of how social media has facilitated the rise of people power include:

- Just moments after Alistair Darling's 24 March budget increased tax duty on cider to 10 per cent above inflation, a Facebook group had been set up to protest about the hike. 'Leave Our Cider' had nearly 250 members within half an hour of the budget announcement, responding to the plaintive, 'What have us cider drinkers done to Alistair Darling?' rallying cry. Within four days, that number had jumped to 45,000.
- After the runaway success of 2009's Facebook campaign 'Rage Against the *X Factor*', which was launched in the run up for

Christmas 2009 with the aim of getting rock band Rage Against the Machine to the coveted Christmas number one spot, instead of *X-Factor* winner Joe McElderry, 2010 saw the anti-*X Factor* contingent upping the ante with a campaign to get experimental composer John Cage's completely silent piece, 4' 33", to the top of the Christmas pops.

- When Keir Moffat, a 26-year-old web designer from Bristol, blew his chance to ask out a girl he'd met on the train back home from Cardiff, he hit on the idea of launching a Facebook group to try to track her down. Within ten days of launching the Mystery Train Girl Facebook group, it had attracted more than 13,000 followers from around the world. Sadly Mr Moffat decided that the mystery girl most likely didn't want to be found and closed down the group, asking followers to donate £1 each to Marie Curie Cancer Care and raising £1,000.
- Findus chicken curry crispy pancakes were back on the menu in April 2010 after 2,000 fans signed up to a Facebook group demanding their return.

The beauty of social-networking groups is that anyone can set one up from the comfort of their own sofa and become an overnight internet sensation. Take Adam Slavick-Lennard, whose sleep talk ramblings were posted on Facebook and Twitter and on the very successful blog The Sleep Talkin' Man by his long-suffering wife, and proved so popular they are set to be made into a book. 'I'm making pillows. Burn them slowly, keeps them fluffy! Mmmmmm, pillows,' is the kind of middle-of-the-night comment that has set the social-networking world afire.

TOP 20 WEIRDEST GROUPS ON FACEBOOK

1 Can this sausage roll get more fans than Cheryl Cole?
2 I Flip My Pillow Over To Get To the Cold Side
3 Bacon
4 Group against Animal Cruelty And Support For Tigers to Wear Rocket Boots
5 My sister said if I get one million fans she will name her baby Megatron
6 When I'm Home Alone and I Hear a Noise, I Freeze and Listen for Ages
7 Petition to Make It Law That Bendy Buses Make Accordion Noises When They Go Round a Corner
8 Panicking When Your Finger Gets Stuck in Something Stupid
9 I Hate It When You Open Your Fridge and Get Punched By a Bear
10 Facebook Group for People with Unusual Head Geometry!!!
11 I Will Go Slightly Out of My Way To Step On A Crunchy-Looking Leaf
12 I Yell at Inanimate Objects
13 I Insult the 'Computer' when It's Too Slow
14 'Let's Eat Grandma!' or, 'Let's Eat, Grandma!' Punctuation Saves Lives
15 Honestly, I Write 'LOL' and I'm Not Even Laughing
16 Pretending to Use the Force to Open Automatic Doors
17 Anatidaephobia -- the Fear That Somewhere, Somehow, a Duck Is Watching You

Facebook Crazes

Social-networking sites like Facebook operate as a kind of large-scale, cyber version of the school playground. If one cool person wears it/plays with it/listens to it then word spreads and soon everyone wants to follow suit. Here are three of the biggest recent Facebook crazes...

1. 'BRA COLOUR'

In January 2010, male Facebook users were left scratching their heads when it suddenly appeared as if every woman was updating her Facebook status with 'black' or 'white' or, less often, 'hot pink' or 'sexy black and gold'. Speculation about what it could all mean was rife until gradually it transpired that it was all part of a campaign to help raise awareness for breast cancer and women had been asked to update their status with the colour of the bra they were wearing that day.

2. 'I LIKE IT ON THE FLOOR'

So successful was the bra colour campaign that Breast Cancer Awareness repeated the concept in October 2010 . Again there was mass bafflement when suggestive updates started appearing such as 'I like it on the washing machine', 'I like it on the stairs', 'I like it in the hall cupboard'. Once again, the collective male Facebook pulse was raised – with 'I like it on the floor' becoming one of the top searched internet phrases – until it was revealed that women had been asked to update their statuses with the place they prefer to leave their handbag.

3. '25 RANDOM THINGS ABOUT ME'

February 2009 saw a rash of strange confessional 'notes' sweeping the Facebook landscape. Former deputy Labour leader John Prescott once bought Tony Blair a goldfish to cheer him up, Nick Clegg ate fried bees in China and was given community service as a teenager for setting fire to a rare collection of cacti. The craze worked along the same lines as a cyber chain-letter, with users urged to create a list of 25 random things most people would never guess about them, and send it on to 25 friends, asking them to do the same thing. The craze went viral with millions of people jumping at the chance to share their innermost secrets with the online world. However, as with most fashions, it wasn't long before the backlash started, with people posting spin-off Facebook groups such as 'Bet I can find 1,000,000 people who are sick of 25 things'.

Addiction

What few people realised until too late is that social-networking can be seriously addictive. Between December 2008 and December 2009 there was an 82 per cent increase in the amount of time people spent on social-networking sites globally, according to a report by media research giant Nielsen, and numbers are still growing.

To put it another way, when it comes to social-networking, we just can't get enough.

We check our profile pages hundreds of times a day, have alerts sent to our phones so we know who's messaging us, and even update our statuses from the toilet.

According to a 2009 survey conducted by US- and Canada-based online measurement service, Crowd Science, 32 per cent of Twitter users say they spend too much time using social-networking sites, 22 per cent say they've written things that they've later regretted, and 16 per cent acknowledge that they often neglect important activities to spend time on social-networking sites.

Psychologist Dr Aric Sigman believes that the time we're spending social-networking, in addition to the 4–5 hours we already spend watching the television, is taking its toll on our ability to form relationships in the real world. 'It's not the social-networking on its own; you're just adding it on to existing screen-watching hours – and there are only 24 hours in the day. That time is lost from somewhere. And we are losing face-to-face time with real people that we love and care about – and limiting what people we could meet and end up loving and caring about.'

CHILD ADDICTS

Despite a 2009 survey conducted by YouGov on behalf of Open Text revealing that 71 per cent of UK workers believe that teaching social media technologies and social-networking in schools is inappropriate, more than half of Britain's school children can't resist accessing social-networking sites during lessons. In 2008 an IT security consultancy called Global Secure Systems (GSS), found 52 per cent of one thousand 15 – 17-year-olds surveyed confessed to looking at Facebook and other networking sites in the classroom. More than a quarter claimed to be facebooking in class for at least 30 minutes a day.

So just how dangerous is all this underage social-networking? In April 2009, top scientist Susan Greenfield warned in the *Daily Mail* (23 April 2009) *How Facebook Addiction is Damaging Your Child's Brain)* that excessive use of social-networking sites could affect the development of children's brains. Some of the reasons she cited as cause for concern were:

- Children's brains are still growing and need to experience the full range of three-dimensional social interaction in order to reach their full capacity. Social-networking in fact limits a child's experience of social interaction in that it doesn't teach children how to interpret voice tone, body language or even how to respond to physical chemicals. This could have a serious effect on a child's future ability to communicate, empathise and to build relationships.
- Social-networking poses a threat to a child's ability to sustain concentration. It is a world of rapid-succession images and instant responses. If children grow up exposed to this sort of activity, isn't there a risk that their long-term attention span might become shortened?
- The practice promotes the idea of immediate gratification. Online sites are all about the here and now, the immediacy of experience. How can children learn about long-term strategy, patience and consequences in that environment?
- Social-networking could potentially interfere with a child's sense of identity. If you use your status update to post details about

every aspect of your life, in the expectation that others will both read and comment on it, isn't there a chance that you might start experiencing yourself increasingly through the eyes of other people and defining yourself through their response, rather than through your own self-knowledge?

Psychologist Dr Aric Sigman believes that, 'With people who are not yet grown adults, the rule of thumb should be that the majority of your life should be in the real world, with a minimum of time spent in the virtual world in terms of relating to people. Up to the age of twenty-four-and-a-half, the stage at which the brain finishes developing, two hours a day spent in front of a screen is enough. Biological changes in your body are still happening up to that time, so if you're spending three hours a day social-networking, you should think about cutting it back.

'Bear in mind, this is against a backdrop where the average adult in the UK spends 4 hours 18 minutes a day watching TV. Given that this is a generation that already spends so much time in front of screens, any addition to that 4 hours 18 minutes, in terms of social networks, DVDs or video games, is too much. Fixing a lower number of hours is better – for example two hours of screen-watching, irrespective of what it is. If they want to spend that two hours social-networking as opposed to watching *The X Factor*, that is fine.

'But it's important for the under-25s to realise that if the time spent social-networking is additional to that four hours of TV, it's likely that social-networking is actively displacing interacting with other people in the real world.'

WOMEN ADDICTS

According to a recent survey conducted by Light Speed Research for Oxygen Media and published in July 2010, 39 per cent of American women who use Facebook are addicted to it. A total of 1,605 women users between 18 and 34 were polled in the survey, which also revealed that:

- 34 per cent said that their profiles on Facebook are the first thing they check upon waking up, even before going to the bathroom, washing their faces or brushing their teeth.
- 23 per cent admitted to sneaking a look at Facebook in the middle of the night.
- 31 per cent of the women said they felt more confident of their online profiles than their real life ones.
- 63 per cent used Facebook as a career networking tool.
- 53 per cent said that they had more online interactions with people than face-to-face encounters.

FRIENDS ADDICTS

Addictions expert Dr David Smallwood was reported in several papers in October 2008 claiming that one in ten Britons could be vulnerable to 'friends addiction' – the compulsion to acquire more and more friends. He recommended that anyone with drug, alcohol or shopping addictions should stay well away from the social-networking website and warned that people could feel severely damaged or isolated when their friend requests are rejected.

The scale of the friendship addiction has become so widespread that the term 'Friend Whore' – meaning someone who sets out to amass as many friends as possible on My Space or Facebook – has become common parlance.

HOW TO SPOT A FRIEND WHORE

1 They block-book friendships – so you'll suddenly see on your news feed that XX is now friends with… followed by a list of 10 or 20 names. This is a clear indication that someone has gone around at one particular social event collecting as many Facebook details as possible.

2 The comments on their Wall often start 'We've never actually met but…'

3 When they post a quiz asking, 'What would XX do in this situation?' or 'Which adjective best sums up XX', no one replies, as so few people actually know them personally.

4 Their friends' list pages run into triple figures.

5 They never post personal details in case one of their 'friends' (most of whom they don't actually know at all) turns out to be dodgy.

TOO ADDICTED TO HIDE

A fugitive from American justice was arrested in Mexico in October 2009 after boasting on Facebook of the exotic life he was leading on the run. Maxi Sopo fled the States in February after he realised that federal agents were closing in on an alleged bank fraud scam that had netted more than $200,000. He was caught when investigators discovered his whereabouts thanks to one of his Facebook 'friends'. US agents made the breakthrough when they came across Sopo's profile on the site. Sopo revealed through his status updates that he was 'living in paradise' and 'loving it' and that we are only 'here to have fun parteeeeeee'. It was while out partying that he met a former Justice Department official and added him as a friend. When agents spotted that one of Sopo's contacts might be on their side they asked him to help locate the fugitive. He obliged and police discovered Sopo living in an apartment complex in Cancun, working at a hotel and partying at the resort's beaches, pools and nightclubs.

5 SIGNS YOU'RE ADDICTED TO FACEBOOK (ACCORDING TO SOCIAL PSYCHOLOGIST, DR ARTHUR CASSIDY)

1 You believe that Facebook has total control over your life and determines ALL your social and leisure activities.
2 You always feel positively reinforced by every single word you type into your Facebook account. In other words, just being on Facebook makes you feel good.
3 You update away without any restraint, disclosing important information about your likes and dislikes, what you are wearing, your emotions – and any aspect of your relationships past and present.
4 You simply can't carry on with your day-to-day work or study until you have logged into your Facebook account.
5 Everyone you know uses Facebook all the time – so you feel you have to be on it to keep up, instead of believing that you're an individual and don't have to be part of the herd mentality.

MY STORY: 'I'M ADDICTED TO TWITTER'

Matt Guest, 29, Consultant

'I'm a Twitter novice, and about a month ago I decided to take the plunge and try it out. I mean, it's where all the papers get their celebrity quotes from so I figured I might as well see what all the fuss was about and create an account. Turns out, until you get into the swing of things, it's quite hard to get your head around, so it took me a few goes to get the hang of it and figure out my @'s from my retweets. However, once I started it was a bit of a Pringles syndrome, I literally couldn't stop. It's even worse because I've got a smartphone so I can check it wherever I am. Strangely it's even more time-wasting than Facebook because there's always something new on it, and whether you end up following a link from Lindsay Lohan to some trashy photo she took of herself or check out the Tate's new exhibition there's always somewhere to go on it. Of course the big thing about Twitter is that you've got to get your sentence out in a word limit. Now this restriction has rubbed off quite badly on me – if I'm really swamped at work and trying to get through a load of emails I, without even noticing, slip into "twitter sentences". It's now been the fifth time I've sent a fairly incomplete sentence to my boss – all receiving very frosty replies asking me to rephrase my email, and last week I did it to a very important client. That didn't go down well and "Sorry I have a serious Twitter addiction" didn't seem to help my cause...

Social-networking to the Rescue

With so many of us ever more reliant on social-networking for friendship, love and entertainment, it's not that surprising that increasingly we're turning to Facebook or MySpace or Twitter for help in times of trouble. In fact, so much are we depending on the restorative powers of social-networking that it is fast becoming the fourth emergency service.

A cursory glance around the millions of status updates at any one time will reveal a huge range of pleas for help from people organising the school cake sale or putting together a historical memoir to those helping out in disaster areas and war zones.

Sometimes, social-networking is even the first port of call in an emergency situation.

STATUS UPDATE: OMG WE'RE TRAPPED!

In September 2009, two girls aged 10 and 12 who became trapped in a storm-water drain in Adelaide, Australia, raised the alarm via Facebook rather than calling the police. Luckily one of their friends was online at the time and alerted the authorities, but the case caused widespread concern among child protection agencies that social-networking has become so big a part of children's lives that they will automatically choose that as a method of communication, even if what they want to communicate is particularly urgent.

THE TWITTERING TRIATHLETE

Twitter came to the rescue of an injured American triathlete in August 2010.

Leigh Fazzina was taking part in a cross-country triathlon when she took a wrong turn while bike racing and ended up lost in a 300-

acre wood. Trying to rush back to the race, Fazzina became entangled with a tree root and ended up hurt. Unable to move, she decided to tweet for help. 'I've had a serious injury and NEED Help! Can someone please call Winding Trails in Farmington, CT tell them I'm stuck bike crash in woods.' Within minutes, some of her thousand plus followers had responded to her distress call and phoned the local fire service and Fazzina was located and rescued.

'THANKS TO TWITTER, RESCUERS DIDN'T GIVE UP'

Eleven long days after the horrifying Haiti earthquake in January 2010, rescuers had all but given up searching when Twitter reports began to emerge of a possible survivor under the rubble of a collapsed hotel. Twenty-two-year-old Wismond Jean-Pierre was trapped in the remains of the hotel shop in Haiti's capital Port-au-Prince where he'd worked. His desperate brother heard tapping from under the rubble and, with the city in chaos and lines of communication down, he asked a local with links to Greek TV to spread the word on Twitter. Rescue teams who were waiting at the airport to fly home, convinced there could be no more survivors, rushed to the scene to pull the relieved hotel worker to safety.

TRANSATLANTIC FACEBOOK RESCUE

A British teenager who took a drugs overdose in April 2009 was saved after the American girl he was chatting to online raised the alarm. Even though the girl, who lives in Maryland, USA, didn't know where the 16-year-old boy lived, she asked her mother to help track him down after he sent her a private message saying he intended to kill himself. Local police in Maryland were called, who then contacted a special agent at the White House and the British Embassy in

Washington. The boy was finally traced to an Oxfordshire address. When police arrived they found he had taken an overdose, but was still conscious.

Diagnosed by Twitter

Not only have people been rescued from treacherous situations by the power of social-networking, they've also been remotely diagnosed through cyberspace, occasionally literally saving their lives, as these stories demonstrate.

FACIAL PARALYSIS

When Marj Beattie from Glasgow read a tweet from graphic designer Patrick Johnson whom she was following on Twitter in August 2010, complaining of a strange feeling on one side of his face, she recognised possible early symptoms of Bell's Palsy, a form of facial paralysis. Though she'd never met Johnson, a Cornwall-based businessman, she left him a message alerting him to the potential problem and he hotfooted it to hospital where Marj's diagnosis was confirmed. Luckily it had been found early enough to respond to treatment.

DIAGNOSIS NAILED

Sarah Lintern was so proud of her newly-manicured nails, she posted a photo on Facebook showing them off, according to The Sun newspaper. She was puzzled when, alongside the expected compliments, she received a brief message from a guy she'd met once or twice at a running club advising her to Google 'Marfan's'. Knowing he was a doctor, she took him seriously and found herself reading up on Marfan's syndrome, a potentially fatal disease characterised by long fingers and limbs and hyper flexibility. Physically, the description matched Sarah exactly and sure enough she was soon diagnosed with the condition, which is a disorder of the connective tissues holding the body together, including the heart. As a marathon runner, Sarah could have triggered a heart attack at any time but thanks to her Facebook diagnosis, she was able to make changes to her life to cut down the health risks.

Cyber-Save the Animals

As we've already seen, social-networking has become one of the most effective ways of modern-day campaigning and nowhere is that more evident than the nation's very favourite type of campaign – to save an endangered animal.

The British can't resist a creature in distress and thanks to the ability of social-networking to get a message across to the largest number of people in the shortest amount of time, and to target those most likely to be receptive, campaigns highlighting the plight of sad, mistreated or threatened animals have been wildly successful.

Such is the impact of social-networking that occasionally, even things that don't start out as a campaign can be turned into one, as in the case of Lowrie the piglet. Lowrie was born in April 2010 at a farmhouse in Shetland, but was the runt of the litter and farmer Heather Davidson had to hand-rear him, keeping an online Facebook diary where she posted pictures so friends could keep up with his recovery. After two weeks, Lowrie's Facebook page had attracted 3000 fans, all desperate to hear what his fate would be, and his owner decided that with such a devoted following, this was one animal not destined for the Sunday roast. In Lowrie's case, Facebook literally saved his bacon.

Theo the cat is another animal who owes his life to Facebook. After an accident in the summer of 2009 left him unable to open his jaw, and facing the prospect of starving to death, his desperate owners were told it would cost £605 for an operation to put him right. Unable to meet the costs, they started a Facebook group to raise the money for Theo's op, and soon had enough to meet the costs of the surgery.

IN THE PAPERS: 'FACEBOOK SAVED MY JOB'

A Facebook campaign in the summer of 2010 to save a popular local lollipop man whose job was threatened because he was reaching obligatory retirement age, was successful after it attracted over 600 members. Sixty-nine-year-old Les Wallwork was initially told he would have to stand down from his job manning a crossing outside Smith Bridge Primary School in Rochdale when he reached seventy. However, after the campaign gained so much support from staff, children and parents alike, the body which manages highway safety for the council agreed to reverse the decision. 'We Saved Lollipop Les' read the revised group name

IN THE PAPERS: 'FACEBOOK SAVED ME FROM JAIL'

A 19-year-old from Harlem had reason to be eternally grateful to his social-networking site after a comment he made on Facebook became his alibi and saved him from being convicted of a robbery he didn't commit. Rodney Bradford posted the update 'Where's my pancakes' from a computer in his father's apartment in Harlem at 11.49am on 17 October 2009 — the exact same time as a robbery was being carried out in which he was later arrested as a suspect. When Facebook confirmed that the update had been typed from his father's Harlem address, the charges against the teenager were dropped.

10

The Language of Social-Networking and Getting It Together

Language Lore

Just as social-networking sites have brought with them their own rules and unspoken etiquette, so they have also been responsible for the evolution of a new type of language. Most of us can just about manage to translate 'lol' or 'omg' (although LMAO or ROFL might prove one step too far), but according to research carried out by PhD student Lisa Whittacker at the University of Stirling and disclosed in April 2010, teenagers have developed a social-networking language of their own, largely due to a desire to keep their Bebo and Facebook conversations private from parents and other adults.

Whittacker identified terms like:

- 'Getting MWI', apparently short for Getting Mad With It (or in other words, drunk).

- 'Ridnick': Feeling Embarrassed (as in, having a red neck – geddit?).
- 'Legal': Being 16 or over and past the age of consent.
- 'Ownageeeeeeee': Being in a relationship.

For those still struggling to keep up with their teen's online speak, here's a glossary of some of the rest of the most commonly used terms:

- Peng: Tasty food or someone good-looking.
- Chung: High.
- BRB: Be Right Back.
- WUUT: What you up to?
- Safe: Goodbye.

It's not only teenagers that have developed their own social-networking code, in 2009 the Oxford English Dictionary made 'tweetups' (gatherings organised through Twitter posts) and 'unfriend' (deleting someone from your friends list) two of their words of the year, after their sudden ascent to popularity due to their place in the social-networking lingo.

Some scientists and social analysts have become concerned about the way they see social-networking sites devaluing the English language as the abbreviations and slang words used by teens are increasingly adopted by the rest of us a) because they're often easier to type and b) because if you hear or read something often enough, sooner or later it becomes the norm. The problems start when people stop being able to differentiate between formal and informal. 'Using this abbreviated type of language can affect the way you present yourself in the workplace,' warns psychologist Dr Arthur Cassidy, 'and if you start using it in a CV, for instance, it won't do you many favours. Similarly, employers are unlikely to be impressed by text language or the sort of language used on Facebook.'

Parties

Because social-networking was created mostly as a way of putting people in touch with each other, it became the obvious place to post information about events. Instead of having to individually post out customised invitations or flyers, you could post up a general invite and know that all your friends would see it. What a result!

What people didn't initially quite grasp was that while all your friends could indeed see it, so could a whole load of people who weren't exactly your friends... and a whole lot of their friends... and a whole lot of their friends and... well you get the picture. Putting information about a party on a social-networking site became tantamount to announcing a free-for-all – with some legendarily unfortunate results...

PARTY POOPERS

When two teenagers from Farnborough decided to throw a party in July 2009 and posted the details on Facebook, it soon got out of hand. One-hundred-and-fifty gatecrashers descended on the quiet residential street, fights broke out and furniture was smashed. Police were called to deal with the partygoers and a helicopter and specialist dog handlers were drafted in. The stepfather of one of the party-givers later blamed Facebook for the way things got out of control, saying that he'd warned the two not to publicise the party on a social-networking site, and that once it's online it's impossible to keep control of numbers. However, 17-year-old host Jordan Wright remained unrepentant, describing it as 'wicked'.

LOST AT SEA

In June 2010, around 500 party-goers attending a rave that had been advertised on Bebo had to be rescued by coastguards from a tiny uninhabited island after they were cut off by the rising tide. They'd walked across the causeway linking Cramond Island on the Firth of Forth near Edinburgh to the mainland but when the evening tide came in and covered the pathway, hundreds of them bombarded the local police and emergency services with calls. Many of the guests were dressed in summer clothes as the weather had been fine when they'd set out in the afternoon, only to turn cold and blustery later on. Some had to be rescued by lifeboats, and around 130 were led by police across the mile-long causeway when the tide went out again for four hours after 1.30am on Sunday. Others were picked up by boat when they were cut off again by the tide at 5.30am. Six had to be treated for hypothermia.

THE PARTY TO END ALL PARTIES

When a group of squatters occupying a £10million Mayfair mansion were threatened with eviction in February 2010, they decided to throw open the doors of their new home for one last shindig – and advertise it on Facebook as a 'Night of Mayhem'. They were expecting a few hundred people at most, but got more than they bargained for when thousands of young people descended on the prestigious address determined to make the most of the night's entertainment. As more and more revellers arrived, police in riot gear descended on the house, concerned about overcrowding inside the five-story building and also outside, where people were swarming over walls and on balconies. The address? Dunraven Street – you couldn't make it up!

Flash Mob

Social-networking, with its ability to connect *immediately* with a mass of people all sharing the same interests, was always bound to revolutionise the way we get together socially, and never has this been more apparent than in the phenomenon of the flash mob. The first flash mob happened in Manhattan in June 2003 when a seemingly random group of people gathered in a carpet store to admire the same carpet. Less than ten minutes later they were gone, much to the bemusement of the sales assistant.

Within a few months flash mobs – mass groups of people who prearrange to meet in a public place and perform a weird, and often completely pointless, act for a short time before dispersing – had spread to Amsterdam, Australia, Brazil and Dublin.

Those first flash mobs were assembled by email, web page and word of mouth, but social-networking allowed the concept to expand beyond anyone's wildest dreams. Suddenly there were flash mobs everywhere – some choreographed to perfection, such as when 200 people walking randomly through Grand Central Station in New York suddenly froze and remained frozen for a few minutes before unfreezing at the same second and walking away, or the hundreds of dancing commuters at Liverpool Street Station performing a coordinated mix of hip-hop, disco and ballroom moves in the middle of one of London's busiest stations (this was screened as a T Mobile advert). Others were more anarchic, with flash mobs assembling to have mass play fights.

There are hundreds of flash-mob groups on Facebook at any one time, but not everyone is thrilled about their popularity. Where police find out about them in advance, many events are called off over health-and-safety fears. Because social-networking isn't an exact science, no one ever knows exactly how many people will turn up. Mass pie fights and pillow fights have all been stopped at the last minute, and a big organised water fight in Leeds in 2008 led to thousands of pounds' worth of damage. When a second flash mob gathered in Liverpool Street Station a month after the first to dance to silent disco, courtesy of individual headphones, the station had to be closed due to overcrowding – over 12,000 people gathered after the event was publicised on Facebook.

11
Reunited – and It Feels Good

Reunions

The good news about social-networking is it puts you in touch with people who you might otherwise have lost touch with. The bad news is… it puts you in touch with people who you might otherwise have lost touch with. The fact is that as we go through life there's a certain element of natural selection. We gain and drop friends as we change both in circumstances and as people. Social-networking puts an end to that. All those friends and acquaintances we might in the normal course of events have outgrown or left behind, can pop back into our lives at any point thanks to the wonders of technology.

Sometimes these reunions are wonderful, cherished events. Newspapers and television regularly report on lovers reunited after 20, 30 or even 40 years, estranged parents finally tracking down their children, adopted children finding the families they never knew – all through the power of social-networking.

However, there's also a darker side to social-networking reunions. Relationships experts have long expressed concern about the speed with which former childhood friends and sweethearts can become intimately involved once put back in contact after a long period of time. There's a tendency to glorify the past, particularly from the vantage of middle or old age, with its dual burdens of responsibility and regret. Everyone wants to be swept up in a love story – and the re-arrival of someone who shares your history and remembers you when you were young and fearless is often an irresistible temptation.

WHY WE LOOK UP OLD FRIENDS ON SOCIAL-NETWORKING SITES:

1 **Curiosity** – will they have lived up to their promise or conversely to their low expectations? Are they still chubby/funny/downright weird?

2 **Nostalgia** – Remember that time you tried to gatecrash that party, or that school trip to Calais? Wouldn't it be great to reminisce with someone who was there, and who remembers you before you became so careworn?

3 **Comparisons** – Have they been more successful than me? Have they aged better?

4 **Settling old scores** – Can't wait to show her how well I've done – after she said I'd never amount to anything. Won't he be shocked when he meets my gorgeous wife – after he always had to have the hottest girlfriends

5 **Boredom** – I never meet anyone new, my life is so routine. Wouldn't it be easy just to click on this 'send' box and find a new ready-made friendship, without having to go through the boring business of meeting people and getting to know them?

MY STORY: 'SHE GOT BACK IN TOUCH JUST TO TRY TO CONVERT ME!'

Ashley Ferrari, 24, Performer

'You get some funny characters on Facebook. Really you do. The strangest are always people from school, people you haven't seen or spoken to since you were eight and they wet themselves in PE class. And yet somehow (and sometimes you really wonder, how did they possibly find me?) they track you down years and years later and it turns out they have four kids at the age of 20 or they've moved to Spain and now live on a pig farm or have turned out looking strangely exactly the same. One of the girls that went to my primary school added me a few weeks ago. I accepted, because I always accept so I can have a snoop around and then when I've checked out their boyfriend and terrible status updates I delete them. This one it turned out had become a bit of a serious Bible Basher; her status was that she 'Will only be checking Facebook on Sundays, and if you'd like a free daily Bible verse to be sent to your phone each day of Lent please text me.' I scrolled down and saw she'd added nearly all of our old class, and the status was completely for us – she was trying to convert us through Facebook, a truly modern Christian way I guess. A day or two later I saw another status saying something about "horrible and very lost (I presume she was talking metaphorically) people" – it looked like the naive move of giving out your number to a load of people you knew 10 years ago and expecting them to hop on the Bible Bandwagon had backfired... Oh dear.'

THE PROBLEM WITH OLD FLAMES...

1 Even if you haven't seen them for decades, there's a tendency to think, 'Oh, I've known him/her for years', which can make you assume an intimacy that isn't actually there.

2 If you knew each other at school or college you'll be tempted to start where you left off, behaving like the teenagers you were when you last met. You might think – at last, someone who knows 'the real me', confusing the 'old', pre-family, pre-career you for the 'real' one.

3 It's easy to get very close, very quickly. Wives and husbands who have been blindsided by a partner suddenly leaving to take up with an old flame they met on a social-networking site, are often shocked by the speed at which it happens – you think you don't need to go through all the getting-to-know-you social small-talk, because of your prior history, although this can cause problems when a love-struck couple suddenly realises they're no longer the people they were back when they first met.

4 Often it's not the other person that we fall in love with but the image of ourselves we see reflected back in that other person's eyes. So, if we're feeling old, past-it, worn-out, it can be a much needed ego boost to know someone else is looking at us and seeing the person we were in our prime, the person we still know ourselves to be underneath.

5 Few things exert more emotional pull than the thought of the paths we didn't take in the past, the doors we didn't open. Given a second chance to rethink the decisions we may always have regretted, make different choices, wouldn't we all be tempted, forgetting that it's the very choices we DO make which shape us into the people we are right now?

REUNITED AND NEVER LOOKED BACK

First there was Friends Reunited – the website which put childhood friends, classmates and sweethearts in touch with one another. Then came MySpace, Bebo, Facebook and Twitter – all of them providing the key to unlock the doors to the past. And we haven't been slow to use it…

MARRIED 30 YEARS LATE

In September 2010, Lynda Cooper married Andrew Blake, 30 years after they split up as teenage sweethearts. The couple met in Worcester when Lynda was just 14 and opened the door to delivery boy Andrew, then 16. They were together two years until Lynda had to move away to Kidderminster with her mother. She never forgot him and for years would send him a blank card on his birthday. Finally, in January 2010, after she had been married and divorced, she got up the nerve to contact him through Facebook and discovered that he, too, was divorced. The couple married 30 years to the day after Mrs Blake first moved away. It was a match made in social-networking heaven.

BLACKPOOL TO BUDAPEST

When Avril Grube's three-year-old son, Gavin, was abducted by his Hungarian father in 1982, she despaired of ever seeing him again. Father and son were supposed to be going to Blackpool Zoo, but instead the boy was taken to Budapest, contravening the terms of a court order. Despite appeals to authorities in England and in Hungary, Avril Grube heard nothing about her son, until her sister came across a Gavin Paros on Facebook in 2009. After a nail-biting wait, he replied to her message and mother and son were finally reunited 27 years after she last waved him goodbye.

SAW HIMSELF, BUT 20 YEARS OLDER

Andy Spiers-Corbett had spent years looking for the father he last saw when he was two. The pair had lost contact following his parents' separation, but though Andy rang every Corbett in Leicestershire, he had no joy in tracing his dad. But when he put the name Graham Corbett into Facebook, he was shocked to find himself confronted with a photo of himself 20 odd years older. The two were finally reunited in May 2010 after 37 years apart and discovered they'd been living just 15 miles from one another all that time.

BROTHER FINDS SISTER AFTER 33 YEARS

Robert Marks was over the moon when he traced his sister on Facebook, 33 years after being given up for adoption as a newborn baby. He had spent 15 years searching for his birth mother, Carol Horridge, finally messaging everyone with the same surname on Facebook. He had almost given up hope when he received a message from someone called Andrea Roczniak saying, 'I think you're my brother'. Mr Marks, who lives in Devon, was thrilled to find his family had also been searching for him, just as he had been searching for them.

REUNITED Case One: 'I reunited with an old school friend on Facebook – and gave him a kidney!'

Medical student Karl Celestine sat down in front of his computer in his family's New York apartment. It was 2007 and Karl was back for the summer from the Dominican Republic where he was studying for a medical degree. Logging onto his Facebook account, Karl noticed he had a new message. He sat upright in his chair when he recognised who it was from. Ricardo Manier – a name he hadn't heard since childhood.

Ricardo, better known as Ricky, had joined Karl's school – the Holy Family Elementary School in Fresh Meadows, Queens – when the two boys were around nine. Before that Ricky had been living in Philadelphia, then California, moving around as his mother's interior design career progressed. Luckily he was one of those kids who settled in quickly wherever he was and he and Karl were soon buddies, going to boy scouts together and playing on the basketball team.

But there was something different about Ricky. From the age of five he'd suffered from nephrotic syndrome – a rare kidney disease which in his case was associated with focal segmental glomerulosclerosis, or scarring on the kidneys. It meant the tiny blood vessels inside his kidneys were leaking, causing protein to pass from his blood into his urine and then out of his body. For as long as he could remember, Ricky's life had been split down the middle. Most of the time, he was a happy, popular, energetic boy who loved sport and being with his friends. But then his face would start getting puffy and he'd start gaining weight – up to 35lbs of water was in his body. He didn't want to eat, he'd feel tired and lethargic, and often he'd end up in hospital, sometimes for a week, sometimes a month.

His new classmates at Holy Family School grew used to Ricky's lengthy absences from the classroom. Sometimes lesson timetables would be altered so that the children could spend a class making cards to try to cheer him up during his long, often mind-numbingly tedious stays in hospital. Occasionally they'd even go to visit him, standing next to his bed, shifting their weight nervously from foot to foot, casting anxious glances up and down the ward, trying hard not to stare.

Karl remembered how pleased they'd all be when he reappeared after these hospital stays. They'd come into class and there he'd be, beaming away at them, looking so much back to his old self that it was impossible not to smile straight back, caught up in his infectious delight in being back in his ordinary life.

The boys were firm friends, soul mates even, until 1996 when, as both boys reached the age of 13, Ricky's family was once again on the move – this time to California. At the time it had been a big blow to Karl, losing one of his best friends. But at 13 it can seem like everything is changing all at once, and Ricky's departure soon faded into the background as Karl began adjusting to life as a teenager in New York.

For a while, the two had stayed in touch, exchanging emails where they'd talk, in time-honoured 'boy' fashion about sport or school, rather than illness or heaven forbid anything emotional. But inevitably, as each developed separate and full lives with new friends and challenges, the email contact grew more sporadic. Ricardo, with his new Californian outdoors lifestyle, seemed like a world away from Karl, back in gritty New York, and eventually, the correspondence petered out completely after four or five years.

Until now.

Fast forward to the summer of 2007, and there's Karl sitting at his computer in his stifling New York apartment, getting a jolt when he sees that familiar name in his inbox: Ricardo Manier.

Eagerly clicking open the message, he read to his delight that his old school friend was once again back in New York City. But his excitement was tempered by concern when he went on to read that Ricky hadn't been feeling too well since being back in his old neighbourhood, and in fact had been in and out of hospital for weeks.

What Karl didn't know is that this time Ricky was seriously sick. It had happened so gradually that he had hardly been aware of it. He'd felt okay, but had started sleeping more and more – up to 18 hours a day.

'You don't look well,' his worried mother kept telling him.

Trouble was, he felt okay – until he developed a severe pain in his foot which was later diagnosed as gout. Once again, Ricardo found himself in hospital. Only this time, the news was worse than usual.

'How on earth are you still walking around?' the incredulous doctor asked Ricky, waving the results of his latest blood test in his hand.

The hospital had assessed Ricky's kidney function by measuring the amount of creatine in his blood. Creatine is a chemical which is a waste product of muscles in the body and high levels indicate that the kidneys aren't filtering waste as they should. Ricky's levels weren't just dangerously high, they were well nigh impossible.

'Another week or so without treatment and you'd have been dead,' warned the doctor.

There was only one possible course of treatment: dialysis. Ever since he was a child, Ricardo and his mum had known he'd have to have dialysis one day, but they'd been hoping to put it off as long as possible. Unfortunately, there was now no choice.

As the rest of New York eased its way into the long hot summer,

Ricardo began a new, agonising regime. Three times a week, he'd get up at 5am and make his way to the hospital where he'd be connected up to a dialysis machine for hours on end, which would basically take over the job of his kidneys for a few hours, accepting the blood from his vein and filtering it of waste, before returning it to his body. 'Surely there has to be another option?' he asked his doctors.

'Only a kidney transplant,' he was told. 'And the waiting list in New York is 10 years long.'

Only if Ricardo found a donor himself would there be any chance of him getting off the hated dialysis, and even then it was far from a sure thing, as the willing donor still had to be a good match in terms of blood types. It seemed impossible.

It was while Ricardo was in hospital on dialysis that he started spending long hours on the internet, trying to make the time pass quicker. Like many people, he'd signed up to Facebook, amassing a sizeable list of 'friends' and he'd spend his time sending messages, or generally keeping up with what they were all doing. It was while he was browsing Facebook that he decided to try out the function enabling users to track down old schoolmates – which is how he came to send a message to Karl.

Within hours, he had a reply. Karl was ecstatic to hear from him, and to know that once again they were back in the same neighbourhood.

'When can we meet up?' he wanted to know.

Then Ricky had to bring his old friend up to speed on his new post-dialysis timetable – the three days a week he spent in the hospital, the agonising slowness with which the hours passed.

'What you need is a night out,' Karl decided after listening sympathetically. They arranged that Karl would come and pick Ricardo up one day after dialysis.

After so much time had passed they were curious as to whether they'd recognise each other, but as soon as Karl set eyes on the guy emerging from the hospital exit, he knew it was Ricky. Taller, skinnier, older, but undeniably the same boy who'd had them all in stitches in the classroom all those years before. Only the paleness of his complexion, and the acne which covered his face betrayed the fact that this was someone who was also gravely ill.

Over a few drinks, the two old friends caught up with everything that had been going on in each other's lives. Karl told an envious Ricardo all about medical school in the Dominican Republic, and Ricardo told how he'd done his pre-med course but would struggle to go on to further medical training because of being tied to dialysis three or four times a week. Under the terms of his health insurance, he had to remain in New York for his treatment.

Then Ricky described what the dialysis was like. Karl, who'd always counted himself lucky to be healthy, listened with growing distress at what his friend had to endure week-in week-out.

From that day, Karl and Ricardo met up every day, becoming like brothers, and it was soon as if the 'missing' decade of no contact had never happened.

One day, when they were chatting, Ricky talked about his dialysis and about how the only chance of getting out of it was to have a transplant.

'I've just got to wait for a kidney to become available,' he explained.

That evening, Karl went home and told his family over dinner what Ricardo had said. His deeply religious mother looked thoughtful. Then she spoke:

'You know,' she said to Karl, 'If you turn out to be a match for Ricky, you should offer to donate one of your kidneys.'

It was the first time that thought had even entered Karl's head, but as soon as his mum made the suggestion, he started thinking 'Why not'? Medical advances had made the operation a lot less risky than it might have been a few years back. Further research on the computer left him even more convinced. Why shouldn't he do it? Why shouldn't he help his friend?

The following day, the two men were driving to a club when Karl turned to Ricky.

'You know, if you need a kidney, I wouldn't mind giving you one,' he announced.

Ricardo was stunned. Ever since he'd started dialysis people had made vague noises about becoming a donor to try to make him feel better, but something about the way Karl looked at him made him realise he actually meant what he was saying.

'All right,' he said grinning, 'let's do it.'

But just because Karl had made the offer, didn't mean the operation was necessarily in the bag. Despite feeling like brothers, the two men weren't related and there was no guarantee they'd be a match. Both tried to downplay any expectations or excitement for fear of being disappointed.

At the end of August 2007, Ricardo made an appointment with his doctor to get his own blood and Karl's tested.

There followed an agonising two-week wait until, finally, the results of the test were in. Despite the fact that they were different blood groups there had been no negative reaction from the blood test.

'Congratulations,' the doctor told them both. 'You're a perfect match.'

At the end of February, 2008, Karl flew back to New York from the

Dominican Republic for the surgery. The two men entered hospital at 5am on 28 February.

Karl would be the first to have his operation. As he sat in his hospital gown, waiting to go into surgery, with his mum and girlfriend close by, the nerves really kicked in. This was a pretty major operation, after all. What if something went wrong? What if he reacted badly to the anaesthetic? What if Ricky's body rejected the kidney and it would all have been in vain?

Making a huge effort to keep these thoughts suppressed, he kissed his girlfriend and his mum, then turned to Ricardo.

'Good luck,' he said.

And then he was lying on the table in the surgery, looking up at the ceiling and the faces of the doctors and nurses.

'We're going to give you something to relax,' he was told. And then everything went black.

An hour after Karl's operation, while he was still unconscious, it was Ricky's turn to say his goodbyes to anxious well-wishers and make his way into the operating room, knowing that when he came to again, everything would have changed.

Because they weren't blood brothers the chances of Ricardo's body rejecting the kidney were significant. Plus, clearly the operation Ricardo was undergoing – removing one kidney and replacing it with another, foreign, one – was much more involved and carried a far higher risk factor, particularly as Ricky had been so sick to start with. As the news came through that Ricky was out of surgery and had been taken to the Intensive Care Unit for observation, all the newly awakened Karl could do was wait.

As the day progressed into evening, the cramps in Karl's muscles grew increasingly uncomfortable and he was given morphine to cope with the pain. Meanwhile in a different part of the hospital, his old school friend and basketball buddy was starting to stir.

Even before Ricardo opened his eyes in the intensive care unit, he was aware he felt completely different. His whole body felt lighter, and somehow clearer. As his overjoyed mum and girlfriend bent over him, they were amazed to see the transformation in him. The acne with which his face had been covered in recent years, had all but vanished. It was like looking at a different man. As he became more and more awake, Ricardo's feeling of incredulity grew. He'd just come through major surgery, and yet for the first time in his life, he felt healthy.

Just two days after surgery, Karl was able to leave hospital. After what they'd just been through together, it felt strange to be leaving Ricardo behind, but his friend was in such high spirits, he knew he wouldn't be long behind him. Sure enough another two days after Karl was discharged, Ricardo too was making his way out through the hospital doors, still marvelling at the change in him since he'd passed through those same doors just days before.

After an early scare, recovery was swift. For the first time in his life, Ricardo was sleeping well and eating well – getting used to a body that functioned as it should.

He and Karl stayed in constant contact, although Karl was anxious right from the start to make sure there was no awkwardness or feeling of obligation getting in the way of their friendship.

'I'm the type of person who, if I want to do something for you, I'll do it and I don't want to hear anything more about it,' he told Ricky soon after the operation. 'So if you want to say thanks, you say it once and then that's it. Okay?'

As Karl, fully recovered, returned to the Dominican Republic to take up his medical studies once again, Ricardo had plenty of time on his hands to think about what he wanted to do with the life that had been returned to him. No longer tied to New York's medical system, he was now free to go wherever he chose – and what he really wanted after the experience he'd been through, was to train to be a doctor himself. The September following the transplant surgery, Ricky few out to the Dominican Republic to study for his own medical degree, and in doing so, he and Karl cemented their existing bonds still further.

Though Rikki has now moved to Boston and married, the two men talk all the time and spend holidays together whenever they can. And both acknowledge they owe a huge debt of thanks to the website which had brought them back together.

'You hear about all the things that can go wrong with websites like Facebook,' says Karl. 'But used the right way, they can achieve incredible things.'

REUNITED Case Two: 'I found my parents on MySpace'

'You know, I might just try putting her name into MySpace or something.'

Sabrina Bailey didn't even need to ask who her 25-year-old husband was talking about. Ever since she'd met Leon, and in fact way before then, he'd been searching for his birth mother, always coming up with different leads, different theories, but all of them had come to nothing.

A few years back, they'd had a brief flurry of excitement when Leon had heard back from the agency in Suffolk, England, which had dealt with Leon's adoption back in the mid-1980s, saying they might have some information. But he'd have had to visit the agency in person, and as he and Sabrina lived in Houston, Texas, with their two little children, there wasn't much chance of that.

But Leon hadn't given up. He'd started putting money by for the trip, and was constantly thinking of new ways of tracing his birth mother – like the MySpace idea.

Scrolling down onto the Find Friends facility on his MySpace account that night in July 2008, Leon typed in the name that was the sum total of what he knew of his birth mother – Debra Kneuman.

At least it's not a common name, he thought for the millionth time as he idly waited for the results to come up. In fact, so unusual was it that chances were he wouldn't find any matches at all.

He was surprised, therefore, when two possible matches popped up on the screen. One was way too young, but the other could be a possibility – except she lived in the States, not in England.

'You've got to write to her anyway,' Sabrina told him. 'It's such an unusual name, there's got to be a chance it's her.'

But when he started to scroll down the page, Leon had another disappointment. Debra Kneuman had last logged onto her MySpace page eight months before. It could be another eight months or even years before she checked in again.

'Go have a look at her friends list,' Sabrina suggested. 'Maybe you could get a message to her through them.'

Debra Kneuman had only one 'friend' on her contacts list – a young woman called Natalie.

'Leave a message for her too,' was Sabrina's advice.

Leon chose his words carefully.

'I'm trying to get in touch with Debra Kneuman,' he wrote. 'If you're in contact with her can you please ask her to check her MySpace page?'

Then came the worst part. The waiting. Finally, three long weeks after his initial approach, he had a message. It was from Natalie, the 'friend' they'd asked for help.

'Yes, I know Debra Kneuman,' she wrote. 'She's my mom. How come you're trying to get in touch with her?'

Leon stared at the screen open mouthed before shrieking: 'Sabrina! Sabrina! I just got a message from a woman who could be my *sister!*'

Sabrina knew just what this meant to Leon. He'd grown up with just one other sibling – an adopted sister. Though his adopted family had always been good to him, he'd felt right from the beginning that he wanted to know the people who'd made him, particularly the woman who'd given birth to him. He'd actually been looked after by her until he was two years old, so he knew there had been a relationship there at one time that he'd somehow been missing all his life.

He'd been told when he was very young that he was adopted. As soon as he was old enough to understand, his adoptive parents had given him a letter his birth mother had asked them to pass on. In it she talked about how hard it had been to make the decision to give him up, and how she hoped he'd now have a better life than she'd have been able to give him. She was just 14 when she'd had him, she told him. She just wasn't ready to look after a child properly.

Leon had always known his natural parents were British. His adoptive parents were Americans but as they were in the military they'd moved around a lot – England, Louisiana, finally ending up in Texas where he still lived.

When he was 18 he'd found some letters relating to his adoption which had given him his natural mother's full name and also led him to the agency which had arranged the adoption all those years before. All these years he'd wanted to find out news of who he was and where he came from, and now here he was looking at a picture of someone who might well turn out to be the sister he never knew he had.

'Send her a message. Quickly!'

Sabrina was almost more excited than Leon. But they both knew they had to be careful. If Debra *was* his mother and she hadn't told her daughter anything about him, revealing who he thought he was might open up a monumental can of worms.

'Can you please ask your mom if she knows anyone by the name of Leon Bailey?' he wrote eventually, adding his number as an afterthought, his fingers trembling as he tapped the keyboard.

Then, just like before, there was nothing else to do but wait.

Debra Kneuman screamed so loudly down the phone, her daughter thought something was seriously wrong. This Leon Bailey guy must be pretty important to have provoked this kind of reaction.

'Oh my God!' Debra gasped, when she could finally bring herself to speak. 'I don't know about the surname, but the only person I know called Leon is my oldest son!'

Now it was Natalie's turn to shriek. Ever since she was a kid she and her two sisters and younger brother had been told about the baby their mom had had to give up for adoption. Their whole lives had been lived in the shadow of the older brother they'd never met.

On his birthday, 12 February, they'd all remember him and wish him happy birthday, and hope that wherever he was, he was celebrating with people who loved him. They'd all dreamed at various points, of finding him, and getting to know him. And now she found out she'd already been in touch with him, without having a clue who he was!

As soon as she put the phone down, she went straight back to the computer to message the mystery correspondent.

'*I'm your sister!!!!!!*' she told him, still scarcely able to believe it herself.

Leon stared at the message, unable to take it in. As he was still trying to digest the news, the phone rang.

'Leon?' the stranger's tone was uncertain. 'It's your mom.'

And within seconds it was as if she wasn't a stranger at all. Over the next 30 or 40 minutes, Debra and Leon caught up on each other's lives. Debra told him all about his brother and sisters and how they'd been wanting to meet him. She told him about how she'd looked after him until he was two, and what he was like as a little boy and how she'd dreamed for the last 25 years of finding him again.

One of the first things she asked him was the question that had been burning into her head and her heart ever since she'd signed away her rights to her son and handed him over to strangers.

'Have you had a good life?'

She was hugely relieved to hear that he'd been cared for and loved, that her sacrifice hadn't been for nothing.

'I didn't know any better,' Debra told him, trying to explain how young she'd been, and how hard she'd tried. 'I just wanted you to have the best possible chance in life.'

When Debra put the phone down on her first-born son, her head was still buzzing.

After all this time, all these years, all the tears, he'd found her *via a website*.

She remembered how naïve she'd been at 13 when she first got pregnant, how little she'd understood of what it meant to be a mother.

She'd been living with foster parents at the time after a turbulent relationship with her real parents. She remembered how fiercely she'd loved her baby, and yet how difficult she'd found being a parent when still only a child herself. She'd been so ill equipped to look after someone else. No one had ever shown her how to do it properly.

She remembered too, Tony Goulbourne, Leon's dad. Tall, handsome, and himself still barely old enough to buy a pint in a pub, let alone become a father. She'd been so bowled over by him, and carried away by how well they got on, not realising that sharing a laugh was a very long way from having a child together. They'd stopped seeing each other by the time she realised she was pregnant and, though he'd tried to hide it, she knew he hadn't been that keen on the idea of becoming a dad.

After Leon was born, Tony saw his baby a few times and, together with his mum, had formed quite an attachment to the little boy, but when Debra had moved down to London with her new boyfriend, they'd completely lost touch. So when – after a few months of struggling with the competing demands of a toddler and a resentful new man – she'd finally realised she couldn't cope, she hadn't even informed Tony that she was putting Leon up for adoption. She'd just assumed he wouldn't be interested.

For 24 years, that decision had haunted her, and she'd wondered where Leon was and whether life had been kind to him. And now, here he was!

Suddenly, Debra felt an overpowering need to find Tony and tell him what had happened. She'd always felt a niggling guilt that she hadn't consulted him about the adoption. When she'd bumped into him in Ipswich a year or so after it had happened and told him about it, she'd been surprised by the flicker of pain that had passed over his face. But she'd never heard anything more from him, so she assumed he'd come to terms with it.

Now though, she wanted to find him again and let him know their son was safe. She'd no idea whether he'd even thought about her or Leon in all these years, but he deserved to know what had happened to their boy. The only trouble was, she didn't have a clue how to get hold of him after all these years. He could be anywhere.

Then she was struck by a sudden wild idea. If Leon had found her via MySpace, wasn't there just a chance, a faint chance, that she could find Tony the same way.

She switched on her computer…

In Ipswich, UK, Tony Goulbourne couldn't understand why his cousins kept ringing him.

'I'm telling you, you've got to look at your MySpace page. There's someone who's really desperate to talk to you.'

At 44, Tony didn't really count himself as one of the computer generation. His kids had helped him set up a MySpace account, but he hardly ever looked at it. He just didn't really get the whole internet thing, and was much more likely to switch on the telly or turn on the music to unwind after a day's work as a senior practitioner, looking after the mentally ill, than start surfing the net.

But his cousin was so insistent, Tony knew there had to be something worth turning on the computer for.

Incredibly, he still remembered his log-in password. Calling up his profile page, he scrolled to the bottom right, where friends can leave messages. He didn't know exactly what he was looking for, but as soon as he saw the picture, he froze. Even after all these years, he still recognised her instantly. Same smile, same eyes. Debbie.

And the second he recognised her, something else also came into his mind. If she was contacting him after all these years, she must have news of their son.

With mounting excitement, he read her message. He was right. Leon had been in touch with her, Debbie told him. He wanted to see Tony. He'd been searching for both of them for years.

As Tony read, a smile came over his face that wouldn't leave him for the rest of the night.

Leon!

The truth is that, as Tony had grown older, he'd come to regret more and more the lack of responsibility he'd shown when Leon was born. In fact, he now viewed that as the biggest mistake of his life. The births of each of his other children – six boys and a girl – had just reminded him of the other son he'd allowed to slip out of his life. He'd told all of them about their eldest brother, and they'd all dreamed of finding him.

When he set up his MySpace profile page, Tony was careful to include the few precious pictures he had of Leon as a baby alongside the photos of his other children. It was his way of saying that he knew he had another son out there, and he hadn't forgotten him – a tribute to the boy he increasingly felt he'd let down.

But now, here was Debbie after all these years, with the news he'd been waiting all this time to hear. Even though he was alone in the house, Tony found he couldn't stop grinning.

Debra had left her number and Tony rang straight away. It had been a quarter of a century since he'd seen her and yet he'd have known her voice anywhere. She was so excited her words spilled out like fireworks.

'I've spoken to him. I've spoken to our son,' she told him. 'He found me on the internet and he wants to find you too.'

As soon as Tony had put the phone down to Debra, he sent a message to Leon using the link she'd given him. Then he spent ages excitedly scouring the photos on Leon's profile page. It was so impossible to equate this man, this father of two, with the little boy he'd held all those years before. And, as for the news that he was now a grandfather, Tony just didn't know how to take that. When his younger brother had become a granddad he'd ridiculed him mercilessly. Now it turned out he was one as well – twice over!

As he was still looking at the photos of his long-lost son, a message came up from Leon. Debra must have let him know they'd spoken. Tony replied immediately, and within the space of half an hour they'd sent several messages back and forth. Then came the phone call – father and son speaking together for the first time. The missing pieces of the jigsaw finally slotting together.

After that momentous night in July 2008, Leon's whole life changed. One by one he made arrangements to meet his birth parents and half brothers and sisters. Debra visited him in Houston not long after making contact, and Leon flew to England in 2009 to spend time with his birth father and his siblings. At time of writing, Tony is making plans to fly out to Houston to meet his grandchildren.

All this time on, Leon still can't quite believe that his years of searching are over.

'I thought I'd be looking all my life to find my birth parents. I always had that worry in my head that something would happen to them before I had a chance to find them, and be able to fit together those missing pieces of the puzzle. I searched for years for them, and in the end they were just a click of a mouse away.'

'Apparently it all kicked off when someone took offence at being defriended.'

12

A Brief History of Social Networking

Ten Stages to Where We Are Today

STAGE ONE: EARLY COMPUTERS AND THE BULLET BOARD SYSTEM

At a time when most of us were still coming to terms with giving up our typewriters for word processors, the early computer pioneers were playing around with the idea of a centralised online 'meeting place', accessed via a telephone line and modem, where users could download files and games and post messages to each other. This text-only exchange of information was conducted at snail-style speed and carried on throughout the eighties and into the nineties.

STAGE TWO: COMPUSERVE

In the late 1980s, CompuServe was just about as hi-tech as you could get. Not only did it allow users to share files and access news, it also introduced to the mainstream the idea of the email and the discussion forum.

STAGE THREE AOL

AOL (America Online) set the online ball rolling by establishing membership-based communities complete with searchable Member Profiles.

STAGE FOUR: SCHOOLS REUNITED

Once the internet was up and running, social-networking started its slow journey into being. In 1995, American Randy Conrads created Classmates.com, an online service aimed at putting people in touch with old school friends. Five years later, Friends Reunited launched in the UK – a site where people could register which school they went to and post information under that school's name about how their lives were going (often using a fair amount of poetic licence!) as well as sending and receiving messages.

STAGE FIVE: SIXDEGREES.COM

A precursor to the modern social-networking sites, SixDegrees.com (1997-2001) was based on the much-reported theory that there are never more than six links in the chain that divide any one person on earth from another (this supposedly stemming from the highly entertaining dinner party game of 'six degrees to Kevin Bacon' where people would try to link any actor to Kevin Bacon in no more than six steps). Users were encouraged to log their likes and dislikes, list their 'SixDegrees friends' and search through the lists of those friends, but the system was complicated and the site closed in 2000.

STAGE SIX: NICHE MARKETING
Services such as MiGente, AsianAvenue and BlackPlanet increasingly allowed users to create professional and personal profiles by specific characteristics, such as gender. Swedish web community LunarStorm added 'guestbooks', friends lists and blogging options in 2000. South Korean virtual world site Cyworld included profile, person search and messaging facilities in 2001.

STAGE SEVEN: WORK AND PLAY
The notion that social-networking didn't just have to focus on people who shared a particular geographical or sociological niche became more widespread with the creation of websites which put people in contact with each other as a way of expanding either their social or their professional lives. Friendster – billed as an online community connecting people through networks of friends – was launched in 2002 by programmer Jonathan Abrams and managed to combine all the better attributes of the sites that had gone before it. Within a year over three million people had registered – which would ultimately prove its undoing as the servers became overloaded and often frustratingly slow. LinkedIn, which was born in 2003, was more about applying the principles of friend-based sites to the world of business, advertising itself as a networking resource for business people wanting to connect with other professionals.

STAGE EIGHT: MYSPACE
MySpace, which also started in 2003, was Friendster's hipper, funkier younger cousin. It gave users total control over content and set itself up as the natural online home for musicians, celebrities, movie buffs,

politicians and anyone else who wanted to establish some kind of individual online identity. The site was funded by ads and soon expanded to include other features such as MySpace IM (instant messaging) and MySpaceVideo (video sharing).

STAGE NINE: FACEBOOK

Those who thought social-networking had reached saturation point after the success of MySpace, were in for a big shock, because nobody could have anticipated the success of its successor, Facebook. Originally founded as a social connections site for Harvard university in 2004 by uber whiz-kid Mark Zuckerberg, its user-friendly features and cheerful graphics meant it soon spread to other campuses, and its targeted advertising made it a magnet for investors.

STAGE TEN: TWITTER

Thinking the world couldn't cope with any more social-connection sites, everyone groaned when the Twitter buzz began in 2006. Ah, but this isn't about connections, it's about micro-blogging – brief updates of what you're up to at any time of the day – said its growing band of supporters. And because the updates are limited to 140 characters, they're necessarily short and sweet, leading to a sense of rapid-fire dialogue, and there are none of the quizzes and 'extras' some people found so irritating about Facebook. It's Facebook for grown-ups, they maintained. Still, in the Facebook-weary late noughties, resistance was high until Stephen Fry single-handedly introduced Twitter to the national consciousness by tweeting a running commentary while stuck in a lift for several hours. The rest, as they say, is social-networking history.

(some source material from 'The History of Social Networking' by Christopher Nickson, digitaltrends.com, 21.1.09)

The Mark Zuckerberg Controversy

Nobody who has seen the controversial movie *The Social Network* can have any doubts that Mark Zuckerberg, the founder of the Facebook empire, has ruffled a few feathers in his relatively brief lifetime. Only 19 when Facebook launched, Zuckerberg's uncompromising style and unwillingness to conform have earnt him some notable critics along the way. The movie focuses on the controversy surrounding the origins of Facebook and the lawsuit brought against Zuckerberg by fellow Harvard students – twins, Cameron and Tyler Winklevoss – who claimed that Zuckerberg had created Facebook using ideas they'd given him when they recruited him to help develop their own social-networking site, ConnectU, and who received a settlement rumoured to be around $65 million.

Zuckerberg was also sued by his former friend Eduardo Saverin, who provided the initial investment for Facebook, but who found himself removed from his official position as co-founder after a disagreement in 2004. The case was resolved in 2009 when Saverin's status was restored.

Zuckerberg's latest civil lawsuit headache involves firewood salesman and web designer Paul Ceglia who, in July 2010, claimed an 84 per cent share of the multi-billion dollar company, Facebook, on the basis that he allegedly signed a contract with the teenage Zuckerberg to develop and design a website, called The FaceBook. Facebook described the case as 'frivolous'.

10 WEIRD AND NOT-SO-WEIRD FACTS ABOUT MARK ZUCKERBERG

1 He describes himself as having a particular talent for 'delayed gratification'.

2 At Harvard, he hacked into university records to prove he could set up an online database of student photos and basic information.

3 When *The Social Network* was released, Zuckerberg followed a priorly-agreed policy of not criticising the movie but indulging it while describing it as 'fiction'.

4 On the day the film was shown for the first time, Zuckerberg appeared on *Oprah* to announce a $100m charitable gift to New Jersey schools.

5 Zuckerberg reportedly shut down the Facebook offices in California, rented out a cinema for the night and took all his staff to see *The Social Network* when it first came out.

6 In September 2010, Forbes magazine named Zuckerberg as the 35th richest man in the US, ahead of Steve Jobs and Rupert Murdoch. He has an estimated worth of £4.4bn.

7 Zuckerberg never finished his Harvard degree, dropping out in his third year to run Facebook.

8 He has been in a long-term relationship with Priscilla Chan, who is taking a medical degree and hopes to be a paediatrician, since before he was famous.

9 The couple rent a modestly furnished home in Palo Alto, California.

10 Zuckerberg has often been called the youngest billionaire, but in fact his former roommate, Dustin Moscovitz holds that honour – he is eight days younger than Zuckerberg and,

because of his long-standing shares in Facebook, he is also a very wealthy man.

'I'm also informed the deceased had over three thousand friends on Facebook.'

13

How Social-Networking Has Taken Over Popular Culture

In much the same way as politicians were quick to cotton on to the power of social-networking sites to shift and mobilise public opinion, so the movers and shakers in popular culture have also been quick to spot the potential in using sites like MySpace and Facebook which are all about social connections, to spread a buzz about a particular artist or film or cultural event and create a word-of-mouth groundswell without the need for expensive marketing campaigns.

Music

Nowhere has the influence of social-networking been more keenly felt than in the music industry. Long gone are the days when people relied on radio to show them what bands were out there, concentrating all the power in the hands of the record labels and the radio DJs. With the advent of social media, the middle people were completely cut out – instead aspiring and established musicians were able to get the music they'd created themselves – often without the need for expensive studio production – directly to their target audience. It was nothing short of revolutionary.

MySpace in particular became synonymous with new user-created music, particularly after the launch of its music profiles in 2004. These profiles were different than the traditional MySpace profile in that they were listed separately from regular users, allowed bands to list their shows, and gave them a way to distribute their music. The site built in a player that allowed musicians to upload songs to their profiles, which users could then access. In September 2004, R.E.M. unveiled their upcoming album on the site, allowing fans to listen to the album online weeks before its release date. Its unique mix of music elements and social-networking made MySpace an invaluable resource for artists wanting direct communication with their audiences. New musicians used their web pages as a launch pad for their careers, and those with an existing fan base were able to interact directly with their fans as well as testing out new material. Bands and solo artists were also able to connect with each other, establishing a musical community invaluable for disseminating information about collaborations, shows and tours.

A number of big-name recording artists have MySpace to thank, at least in part, for their meteoric rise to success. Lily Allen started off by posting demos of her music on the site. Once she was established, she also helped Kate Nash kick-start her career by recommending her music on her page.

Inevitably, the recording industry suffered. Many retail stores closed down and mainstream acts lost popularity as fans were able to find niche acts that catered specifically to their musical tastes.

MySpace wasn't slow in capitalising on its position in the music marketplace. In 2005, it created its own record label – the imaginatively titled MySpace Records. This was followed by MySpace Music, which launched in 2008 in the States and 2010 in the UK – an advertising-supported music and video streaming service conceived in conjunction with the four biggest music labels: Warner, Sony, Universal and EMI. Users could listen to music for free and create play lists which could be posted onto their profiles and shared with friends, but anyone wanting to download songs onto their computers would have to pay.

But MySpace is just the tip of the iceberg. As social-networking continues to expand, more sites are developing their musical platforms. In September 2010, Peter Lawrence, founder of the Big Chill festival, launched Pic-Nic, a subscription-based social media site with an emphasis on music, where user privacy is paramount. 'What we are trying to do is put the heart and soul back into online music communities,' said Lawrence. 'People need a place where they can enthuse and discover and they are doing it for the love of it, rather than the profit factor. Music is too important to be left in the hands of the music business.' September also saw Apple launch Ping, a purely music-based social-networking site integrated into the latest version of iTunes which lets users follow their friends and favourite artists to discover what music they're talking about, listening to and downloading. Soundcloud is another social network where artists can share music, while veteran musician Midge Ure's Tunited offers musicians the facility to sell their tracks in a personalised Tunited shop and build a community around their music. Tunited membership also allows artists access to music software and music industry guidance.

(some source material from 'The Effects of MySpace on the Music Industry', Professor Lance Strate)

AT-A-GLANCE SOCIAL-NETWORKING FOR WANNABE POPSTARS

MySpace: Offers the greatest variety of content for an aspiring band to showcase its music and videos as well as the possibility of customising the flash profile to make it look more professional.

Facebook: There's a tendency for artists to be snobbish about Facebook but its sheer size and ubiquity means aspiring musicians would ignore it at their peril, if only as a platform for promoting gigs and CDs and forming a fan-base.

Twitter: A great place for marketing a brand – and a band!

THE X FACTOR

The hit TV talent show has a love-hate relationship with social-networking sites. On one hand, sites like Facebook and Twitter do a fantastic job of keeping the *X Factor* buzz going. Twitter's list of 'trending' subjects is invariably topped by *X Factor* discussions for a few days following the weekend's contest as viewers debate everything from the judge's outfits to the musical merits of the most recently departed contestant. However, it's social-networking which is also responsible for the anti-*X Factor* backlash which has been gaining momentum over the last couple of years. Fed up at the way some people think *X Factor* guru Simon Cowell has monopolised and manipulated the music industry, various Facebook groups have been set up to garner popular support around organised campaigns aimed at undermining the *X Factor* stranglehold on popular culture. In 2009, The 'Rage Against the Machine For Christmas No 1' Facebook campaign successfully prevented Cowell from securing *X Factor* winner Joe McElderry guaranteed top position in the Christmas charts. In 2010, Cowell-detractors again harnessed the might of Facebook behind a campaign to keep wild-card contestant Wagner in the competition, despite Cowell's ill-concealed impatience with the eccentric Brazilian's ever more colourful performances.

Film

It used to be the case that reviewers led the way in influencing a film's box office success, but more and more, social media is taking the role of arbiter of public opinion. Media analysts point to the fact that movie studios are increasingly ploughing their marketing budgets into ensuring a film garners the best possible box office sales during the opening weekend, so they're investing heavily in social media campaigns to try to drum up that pre-premiere buzz. *Hot Tub Time Machine*, for example, benefitted from a well-orchestrated online exposure, but other films have been less successful. the *LA Times* recently reported the findings of two social computing scientists from HP Labs in California who claimed that analysing Twitter feeds could predict 'with as much as 97.3 per cent accuracy, how a movie will perform on its first weekend of release.'

Hollywood has been quick to seize on the mass appeal of social media. The red-carpet premiere of the second *Twilight* movie was streamed live to millions, boosting the popularity of the film and the franchise. Similarly, 20th Century Fox organised an entire day to promote *Avatar*, holding special 3D preview screenings of footage, and trailers which were heavily promoted via Facebook and Twitter. It was a huge success with all tickets gone in a matter of hours and helped create a buzz around the film which paid dividends at the box office. As the Hollywood studios have found their way around the social-networking phenomenon, they've become increasingly adept at using it for their own ends. They realised early on that the challenge of social media is to engage audiences directly by making them feel like they have a stake in the film, rather as shows like *X Factor* encourage viewer voting in part to make the viewer feel a sense of ownership of the programme, and consequently a vested interest in seeing it through. So marketing departments have focused on the interactive nature of movie releases, coming up with innovative campaigns which encourage active participation, like treasure hunts and online games.

FILMS ON FACEBOOK

Harry Potter and the Deathly Hallows – Part 1
The trailer for *Harry Potter and the Deathly Hallows – Part 1* went live simultaneously on Yahoo! International and the film's Facebook page, showing how movie bosses now put equal emphasis on traditional marketing and social media. The trailer on Facebook incorporated a live chat feature so fans could discuss it.

Sex and the City 2
The digital marketing agency behind the film encouraged cinemagoers to 'Tweet their feet' (in other words to send in photos of themselves in their highest, most Carrie-like heels), leading the film to trend on the social-networking site Twitter

during its opening weekend. The movie also boasted the UK's biggest film page on Facebook, with over 150,000 fans.

Television

With telly being traditionally the 'medium of the people', it's not surprising that it has forged strong links with social-networking – the new 'voice of the people'. Not only do TV insiders use social-networking to publicise and promote their programmes, ordinary users also use Facebook, Twitter, MySpace and all the other social media as a forum to discuss what they've been watching. Obviously, television analysts keep an eye on what fuels the most debate, and that feeds right back into the kind of programmes that get made, and so the cycle continues...

The good thing about social-networking and television becoming intertwined is that we get more say in the kind of programmes that get made, and when we're unhappy about something, we can voice that unhappiness and sooner or later someone will take notice.

The bad thing, at least from the television bosses point of view, is that there's a danger that television will become too populist – responding to what people want, rather than leading the way with trailblazing programming. Also, the idea of the actors interacting directly with the public is a bit of a double-edged sword – while it means they build up loyal fan-bases, it also increases the risk of them saying something indiscreet, without clearing it first with the powers that be – such as when Paula Abdul chose to announce she was leaving the judging panel of *American Idol* via Twitter.

The blurring of the line between social-networking and television is due to get even more pronounced in the near future as Social TV comes into the mainstream. This is where people exchange opinion live online about the TV programmes they're watching at that moment. It sounds like it would be a distraction, but fans insist the extra interactive element adds to the viewing experience, turning TV-watching from an isolated spectator sport to a bonafide social event. Some TV companies are already integrating Facebook and Twitter into their TV systems with onscreen keyboards so that people can tweet from their television sets.

Documentaries are one strand of television programme-making that has benefited hugely from the social media boom. Canny documentary film-makers are able to monitor online chatter before the programme airs and get a feel for which communities have an interest in the subject matter, and invite them to special screenings, or encourage them to post comments.

TAKING A GAMBLE ON SOCIAL-NETWORKING

Bookmakers have been getting worried by the idea that internet analysts could analyse the traffic on social-networking sites like Facebook and Twitter to gauge the popularity of contestants on reality TV shows where the public gets a vote, such as *Britain's Got Talent* or *Big Brother*, and predict the eventual winner. They are concerned that by measuring how much different contestants are mentioned and whether the comments are generally favourable or not, canny analysts could make fairly accurate assumptions about how the public will vote, which could be disastrous for the bookies.

'I see you've created an online alter ego.'

14

Business Social-Networking, Being Someone Else and Are You Online Happy?

Schmoozing

Sites like Facebook and Bebo are usually thought of in a social context – as ways to connect with friends, or with people we'd like to be friends – and normally as being at odds with the world of work, where people sneak glances at Facebook when they should be preparing urgent reports. But we're gradually cottoning on to the benefits of social-networking as a business tool.

Top of the list of netWORKing sites is LinkedIn, a website which lets users build a professional profile and make work connections as well as post recommendations of their skills by other users. According to marketing research company ComScore, which provides data to internet businesses, LinkedIn attracted 50 million users worldwide in July 2010, nearly nine-and-a-half per cent of the social-networking market, with UK users second on the list for spending the most hours on the site.

HELP! I'M A FACEBOOKAHOLIC

While many companies remain nervous of social-networking, regarding it as at best a distraction and at worst a vehicle for expressing employee dissatisfaction, some forward-thinking companies are actively embracing it. In the States, sites like Salesforce Chatter – an in-house networking site built on the same principle as Facebook, where employees can openly interact and share information and build up an online presence within the company – are being hailed by employers as an invaluable way of keeping an eye on the hidden dynamics of a company, and finding out who the real power-houses are.

How Facebook can improve your job prospects:

A thoughtless comment you've left on Facebook can cost you a job interview. Or the job itself. And having the wrong friends can also put doubt on your worth to an employer. So make sure you manage your online Facebook reputation correctly by following these tips from Toni Cocozza, Managing Director and founder of DP Connect, a major IT recruitment company.

- Aim to build a network of contacts that you really trust – and that know you really well.
- Remember, if it's a choice between you and someone else for a job, your Facebook profile or page could tip the balance in your favour – or let you down big-time!
- People are usually on their 'best' behaviour in a face-to-face interview situation. Aim to be exactly like this on your Facebook or social network pages if you want to impress prospective employers.
- If you are actively looking for a job, make sure you check your

Facebook page once a week, keeping everything bang up-to-date.

- Don't think that because there's not much on your CV in terms of work history and skills, a prospective employer won't check your social-networking pages. Many employers now do this kind of check as a matter of routine.

- Comments about the fact you are looking for a job and the sort of career you're hoping to find are fine – provided they're worded carefully to show that you are both professional and discreet.

- It's good to be sociable. Employers usually want outgoing people who can communicate well. But what they don't want are people who loudly proclaim, 'I love everyone, that's why I'm a party animal' or are indiscreet about their views and opinions.

- Less can sometimes be more. A profile that gives key information but says very little can sometimes be better than a badly worded profile that spills the beans about anything and everything.

- You can use Facebook as a mini job-ad. Tell your friends what sort of job you are looking for in a couple of carefully worded sentences. Include things like why you believe someone should employ you and what your workplace skills offer – but avoid mentioning your skills in the bar or the pub.

- If you're already working, keep ALL your comments about work and your colleagues professional and factual.

- Avoid setting out your opinions on anything to do with the workplace. An employer could wind up viewing such comments negatively.

- Think ahead: clever social-networking can always win you valuable contacts, if not for now, then for the future.
- Employers have to compete for the best talent. But that doesn't mean they appreciate derogatory or derisive comments about your previous bosses or your existing company.
- What employers look for are people with skills, enthusiasm and the ability to work hard as well as being discreet – people who can promote the company positively. They definitely don't want people who mouth off at any opportunity about everything under the sun.

Alter Egos

One of the great things about social-networking sites is that they allow us to become whoever we want to be. Although the creation of fake accounts is widely prohibited, people can nevertheless find ways to project themselves as other than who they really are. Shy, retiring types can create flamboyant, extrovert online alter egos who Poke perfect strangers and join every group going; men can find out how it feels to be women for a while; nobodies can turn themselves into celebrities and you can even, as we've already seen, choose to become your favourite pet, should you wish to.

There are many reasons people decide to become someone else on a social-networking site:

- They want to snoop on someone's page without that person actually knowing who they really are.
- They are hopelessly under-confident about themselves.
- They feel like being famous/rich/feline.
- There's something that stops them revealing who they

really are – maybe they're wanted by the law, or by a trail of furious exes.

BEING SARAH PALIN

In August 2009, scriptwriter Alex Grossman was quoted in the *Wall Street Journal* talking about his decision to pass himself off as Sarah Palin on Facebook. Having tried a variety of aliases, he finally settled on the Facebook name Governor Palin. He used a photo of Palin sitting in a car, with an opening message that read 'Happy 4th of July and God Bless!' and was soon bombarded with friend requests from those who genuinely thought he was Governor Palin. Grossman became very diligent about his alter ego, updating his page often with homely, God-fearing messages like 'I need a salmon recipe for tonight. Todd just brought home a fresh one. Something spicy!' (Dozens of 'friends' sent recipes in response) or 'GOD LOVES US ALL, no matter how black or African, or even gay or Jewish we are.'

At the height of 'Governor Palin's' popularity, Grossman had more than 600 'friends' but one day in August 2009, he tried to sign on to the site but was greeted with an 'Account Has Been Disabled' message. Facebook authorities had apparently been alerted to his alter ego's page, decided it was against rules as it constituted a false identity, and closed it down. The governor's private attorney, Thomas Van Flein, was quoted in the *Wall Street Journal* as saying:

'Every day Governor Palin deals with individuals, politicians, and corporations pushing fake and inaccurate information into various media. She believes strongly in the efficacy of using direct web-based communication forums like Facebook and Twitter to reach her supporters, the media, and the public at large. Maintaining the integrity of these forums is obviously fundamental to this new type of interactive communication. With that in mind, we greatly appreciated Facebook's prompt response in disabling the impostor site.'

MY STORY: 'JUST CALL ME FLASH...'

Thomas Logan, aka. Flash Logan, 24, Teaching Assistant
'I have a Facebook alter ego. His name is Flash Logan. He only appears completely intoxicated and wearing sunglasses. Other additional elements have in the past included a hat I found, a cape, and wellies. His profile's pretty popular. He's tagged in a good a hundred or so pictures – and he's got about a hundred friends too. He started at Leeds Festival, but he's surfaced many other places since. Some people only ever meet Flash Logan; they probably don't even know Tom exists.'

Happiness

Does social-networking make you happier? It may sound like a rhetorical question but there are plenty of people who believe that the answer is 'yes'.

Scientists Nicholas Christakis and James Fowler carried out research to find whether happiness is contagious within social networks in the real, rather than virtual, world, and concluded that real-life social networks contain clusters of happy or unhappy people (happy people towards the centre of the network, and less happy on the outskirts), and that we are affected to some degree by the happiness of our friends, our friends' friends and our friends' friends' friends – in other words, those people three degrees of separation from ourselves. They decided to find out if this applied to *online* social networks as well and examined a group of 1,700 college students who were interconnected on Facebook, looking at their profiles, their friends and most importantly, their photographs. The photos not only gave away information on the closeness of connections between the group (the average student in their study had over 110 friends on Facebook, but average of only six 'picture friends' – people close enough that they tagged each other), but also gave clues into their levels of wellbeing. The results showed that those who smile were more likely to be at the centre of the online network than those who don't, emulating the results in society in general.

But social-networking is about more than just 'catching' happiness from your online friends.

A 2010 report by the British Computer Society Chartered Institute for IT found that online social networks had a positive impact on personal satisfaction, particularly within the first two years of an individual becoming 'connected' in this way.

DOES FACEBOOK BOOST WELLBEING?

Wellbeing is most often defined as a feeling of happiness and contentment and feeling good about your life. Mark Millard of Wellbeingwizard.com insists that, according to this definition, social-networking sites like Facebook definitely enhance wellbeing.

'Part of our sense of wellbeing is the quality of our relationships. So social-networking can have a big influence on this. Emotions, for instance, can move through social networks – just like a virus moves through physical networks. And although you aren't meeting people face to face, the emotions you express online can move through the networks just the same. Also, people pick up on what you are saying or doing online. So using this effectively can increase your wellbeing.'

Here are Mark Millard's tips to increasing your wellbeing and happiness through social-networking:

USE HAPPY WORDS

Sounds simplistic, but if you put lots of happy, positive words on your site, you will make other people feel a bit happier. Conversely, if you put lots of negative words you will make them feel negative. So if you use certain words or phrases you can spread happiness via anything that sounds positive, bright, smiley and upbeat. Even if something bad happens to you, talk about it in positive terms, i.e. as a learning experience. Using happy words is an excellent technique for getting into a positive frame of mind.

Here are some suggestions:

It feels fabulous

I feel confident

I think you're right

I feel happy for everyone involved

I feel motivated

It's much better now

I can do it

I'm blessed

I feel beautiful
I love life
I'm inspired
It feels great.

PROXIMITY STILL MATTERS
Actually being with people and doing things is still important. Social-networking facilitates closeness with our connections and our three or four really close friends are very important.

PUT QUALITY BEFORE QUANTITY
Be discerning and careful whom you connect with: just because you can connect with anyone doesn't mean it's always a good idea.

DON'T TRY TO HIDE
Don't think you can 'hide' in social-networking by using a different persona for a different network; some things can cross networks and follow you through time.

FOCUS ON WHAT REALLY MATTERS
There's no such thing as a 'good' or 'bad' place in your network, what really counts is what is going through the network. So continue to choose your friends with care.

NETWORKING IS SOCIALLY VALUABLE
Your networking carries value to you socially. It can give you emotional support and practical help too if you should need it.

DO AS YOU WOULD BE DONE BY

Always behave towards other people in ways you would like them to behave towards you. And don't behave towards them in ways you wouldn't like!

NETWORKING HAS A DIRECT EFFECT ON YOU

Remember that what happens in your network directly affects your wellbeing and happiness. Different things ripple and spread in different ways. Always be aware that the network has memory and moves all the time – just like a living thing.

'Think of an essay as a collection of tweets, only joined together.'

15

Advertising, Hoaxes and Games

Advertising

Advertising and social media are an awkward combination. Facebook's targeted advertising, where over-forties are liable to be hit with ads about tummy-tucks, and over-fifties with competitions to win a Stanna stair lift, leave many people feeling unsettled. How much do they know about me? is a common question. Why do they keep asking me if I want to lose my belly fat? is another.

Where advertising and social-networking seem to work best with each other is in the area of promotional campaigns, rather than one-off ads for specific products. Advertisers are becoming increasingly creative in how they approach the idea of building awareness, whether it's for a brand, a TV programme or even a public service.

So integral has online marketing become to brand recognition that agencies have sprung up which just deal with digital campaigns – like successful digital engagement agency, Holler.

Chris Lane, one of Holler's planners, reckons the reason social-networking is so invaluable in brand promotion is that it is instantly accessible, and the site's very nature makes interaction between consumer and supplier appear friendly and even personal.

'One of the things I think social media is great at doing is reducing the perceived size of a brand. That to me is one of the hallmarks of brands using social-networking platforms effectively. Take a brand in the US the size of Best Buy and you can make it feel smaller, more approachable and capable of having one-to-one conversations with its customer base.

'You could argue this is one of the factors that made the Old Spice campaign so great. Old Spice is a huge brand, but by making it so that members of the public could send in their questions to "The Old Spice Guy" and get personal responses, meant that suddenly the perceived size of the brand shrunk. It felt far less like an unfeeling corporate monolith than before the campaign. It has reduced its "perceived size".'

The key to running a successful social-networking promotional campaign lies in getting the timing right. 'Specific campaigns have got to be timely,' says Chris Lane. 'Trying to build conversation and buzz around something that has no current cultural relevance is a real struggle. Look at something like Nike's "Write The Future". Not only did it have beautifully ambitious content, but in the run-up to the 2010 World Cup, the Facebook page was releasing super timely content and video shorts featuring players that would be playing in games 20 minutes after the video's release. Smart, timely, serving their target audience… it's clever on so many levels.'

Holler's marketing manager, Andrew Vincent, says a successful social-networking campaign should.

GIVE USERS A REASON TO TAKE PART

'For too long it has been enough to merely create a profile and post sporadic, one-way messages without a real direction or reason. The best social media campaigns encourage the participation of their users, whether that's through an amazing piece of content that they activate or a dressed-up piece of market research that allows a user to feel like they are part of the brand. It's all about engaging the user on a two-way basis.'

FLATTER THE USERS' INTELLIGENCE

'Some of the most successful social-networking campaigns give users exclusive insights into what really makes a brand by identifying why a user identifies with them in the first place, playing on their "intelligence" for *choosing* that brand.'

UNDERSTAND ITS AUDIENCE

'While we often try to move away from the strict advertising message, it's still true that an understanding of your audience and, in turn, an understanding of why your audience *might* choose your brand, is integral to a campaign. It's not just a case of offering them a free iPad/Blackberry/Holiday/CD with every question answered because in most cases, once they have their free item, they'll forget who gave it to them. A great example of a campaign that understands its target audience is Adidas' MiCoach. Not only do they clearly see why their users choose Adidas (sports and training), they identify a problem (they aren't helping them in sports and training beyond providing the basic equipment), so they give them the tools to improve themselves (mobile apps and bespoke hardware) and the place to share (the MiCoach community). Which neatly leads to the fact that "social networks" and "social media" **do not** just mean Twitter, Facebook and forums. Social media is everywhere; the medium is just the tool to get in touch.'

Hoaxes

Because they're designed to facilitate instant communication and interaction, social-networking sites are a gift for hoaxers and false rumours which can be spread virally and incredibly quickly. Some of the most popular Facebook hoaxes/fake rumours include:

1 **'Facebook is going to start charging for membership'**. This does the rounds fairly regularly, but luckily has no basis in fact.
2 **'Get loads of free stuff'**. Well, after you've spent ages filling in a complicated survey, before realising that what you actually get doesn't quite match up to what you thought you'd been promised. Oh, and after you've had to invite your entire friends' list too…
3 **'Watch this FANTASTIC video'**. After you've completed yet another survey (and recommended it on everyone's news feed).
4 **'Find out who has been viewing your profile'**. Well, after you've invited all your friends to join and at least 50 per cent of them have accepted… Oh, and even then it won't work. Sorry.
5 **'Do not accept a friend request from XX, he is a hacker and will figure out your computer's ID and address. Cut and paste this message to everyone on your friends' list'**. Or don't bother, because it's actually a hoax, and it isn't actually possible…

THREE TWITTER HOAXES:

1. SARKOZY AFFAIR RUMOUR

In March 2010 unsubstantiated reports started circulating on Twitter about tit-for-tat extramarital affairs involving the French President, Nicolas Sarkozy, and his wife, Carla Bruni. Though the rumours were later thought to have been a hoax started by a French trainee journalist wanting to see how fast Twitter gossip could spread to mainstream news, they spread rapidly all over the world. Only in France itself, with its stricter privacy laws, was the Sarko rumour not discussed in the mainstream media.

2. AIRPORT BOMB JOKE

When trainee accountant Paul Chambers sent out a tweet in January 2010 threatening to blow up Doncaster's Robin Hood Airport – closed due to snow – if it didn't reopen in time for him to fly to Belfast the next week, he thought he was just making a joke. What he didn't think was that his Twitter jest would wind him up in court! Chambers was due to fly to Ireland to meet up with a woman he'd been chatting to on the internet. Frustrated at the thought that the airport might still be shut, he tweeted 'Robin Hood Airport is closed. You've got a week and a bit to get your s**t together, otherwise I'm blowing the airport sky high!'. A member of the airport's management team spotted the message and reported it to the police, and Chambers found himself arrested by the anti-terrorist squad. In May he was found guilty of sending a menacing electronic communication and fined £385 plus £600 court costs – a conviction he later appealed.

3. JOHNNY DEPP CAR CRASH HOAX

Reports of a fatal car crash involving heart-throb actor Johnny Depp began circulating on Twitter in January 2010. The rumour had started when someone came across a fake CNN report on the net giving details of the supposed car crash next to a photo of a smashed car (which later turned out to have been posted on a car buying website) and began tweeting it as if it were fact. Within hours, 'RIP Johnny Depp' became one of the site's trending topics, but fortunately for Depp's millions of fans, he was soon able to quash that rumour in person.

Games

Social-networking sites like Facebook are famous for addictive games. Users are likely to log on to find they've been eaten by killer zombies or had a problem with their crops or landed themselves in trouble with the mafia.

SCRABBLE

One of the great successes of the early days of Facebook was Scrabulous, a plug-in word game which quickly became one of the top ten most downloaded Facebook applications, with over 600,000 daily active users.

With Scrabulous's popularity increasing at a rapid rate, lawyers for toy makers Hasbro and Mattel, makers of the original Scrabble game, mounted a legal challenge in 2008, claiming that the Facebook version was infringing on their copyright. Despite sparking protests by thousands of Scrabulous fans around the world, the game was eventually removed from Facebook, with a fully-licensed version of Scrabble by Hasbro appearing on the social-networking site soon after.

The enduring popularity of the Facebook Scrabble application has come as a surprise to many who had long predicted that social-networking would usher in the end of literacy as we know it.

Not only do millions play online against friends and family, they also have the option to play against total strangers, which has led to a whole Facebook sub-culture of Scrabble romances, Scrabble friendships and even Scrabble 'sex', where players make the kind of words not usually encouraged in a family board game.

MY STORY: 'I MET MY BOYFRIEND PLAYING FACEBOOK SCRABBLE!'

Karen Lewis, 45, Chef
'After I split up with my husband a couple of years ago, I became addicted to playing online Scrabble. The first thing I did when I got up in the morning or came home from work at night was log into Facebook to see what was happening. I always had several games on the go at a time, and I played against total strangers (mostly because my friends were fed up with me getting too competitive!) using the facility it offers to invite random people to play who just happen to be online at the same time and looking for a game. If you've never played online Scrabble, there's a thingy at the side where you can make comments as you play, a kind of chatting, and I struck up 'friendships' with several of the people I played and used to play them regularly. One of them was a guy called James. We started off just commenting on the game, things like "grrrr, no vowels", so hardly the most

scintillating conversation, but we soon graduated to talking about more personal things. I found out he'd recently split up from his long-term girlfriend and we commiserated with each other about how crap it all was. At the time I was playing against people from all over the world, so it was a result to find out that James only lived about 45 minutes away from me, and after a few months of "chatting" we arranged to meet at a motorway service station halfway. I wasn't expecting romance – I just thought we might be able to cheer each other up as mates – but as soon as I saw him hovering uncertainly outside the entrance, my heart just somersaulted. It was the strangest thing. That day we spent three hours talking and within a month we'd moved in together. It really was that quick. I can't believe I found James on Facebook – it's like a lovely dream. And the great thing is that we don't need to go online to play Scrabble anymore! I feel like I've got my life back.'

FARMVILLE

FarmVille is the most popular application on Facebook, attracting between 16 and 17million users a day. A cartoon-like universe in which players build and maintain their own farms, rear live-stock and tend crops, it can be played for free, but players can also buy virtual items and extra virtual coins with real cash – which can sometimes lead to problems. In March 2010 a 12-year-old boy ran up bills of £900 on FarmVille, first using his own savings then his mother's credit card – without her knowledge. At around the same time a councillor in Bulgaria was sacked after he was discovered milking a virtual cow on his laptop during a committee meeting.

16

Things You Never Thought Of, What Not To Do, Doing It Right and Liar Beware

Bet you didn't know you could use social-networking to…

WRITE A NOVEL

When Matt Stewart couldn't find a publisher for his novel, he started posting it on Twitter, one tweet at a time. Starting in July 2009, Stewart reckoned it would take him approximately 3,700 tweets to transmit all of the 480,000 letters in his novel, but it was worth it for the instant feedback from readers, which could be used to develop the characters and plot twists.

TRAVEL THE WORLD

Gateshead man, Paul Smith, set off on 1 March 2009 to see if he could travel across the world to New Zealand in 30 days, using only travel and accommodation offered to him on Twitter. Calling himself the Twitchiker, Paul set ground rules that he couldn't make plans more than three days in advance or stay in one location longer than 48 hours. His trip took him to Amsterdam, Paris, Frankfurt, New York and Los Angeles among other places, restoring his faith in human nature as he went. And right at the end, Air New Zealand came up trumps with an offer to fly him back to the UK.

GET OUT OF JAIL

James Karl Buck, a journalism student from California, tweeted the one-word message 'Arrested' from his mobile phone after being arrested covering an anti-Government protest in Egypt in April 2008. The messages and subsequent tweets were picked up by colleagues in the US and bloggers in Egypt, who were able to galvanise support and find contacts who could help with getting Buck released from police custody. As he left the station, he tweeted one more one-word message: 'Free'.

COMMUNICATE WITH YOUR UNBORN BABY

Proud parents-in-waiting used to have to wait until their baby's birth to hear from it, but thanks to a new invention – Kickbee – they can keep up with their unborn offspring through the pages of a social-networking site. Kickbee – a stretchable band with sensors – transmits a signal via Bluetooth to a user's online profile whenever the baby moves inside the womb. Thrilling updates might include messages such as 'I kicked Mummy' followed by a date and time. Kickbee was invented by researcher Corey Menscher, who set up a Twitter account in the name of his unborn baby, Tyler, which attracted more than 600 followers.

QUIT SMOKING

Increasingly, people are turning to social-networking to help them give up the fags. Facebook has a number of very popular Quit Smoking pages and groups, as well as a fair smattering of 'if 1m people join this group, my mum will give up smoking' type of pages. Many long-term smokers find the instant support which social-networking provides a real help when giving up. Being able to go online at any time of the day or night when your resolve is weakening and being able to talk to other people in the same boat, is an invaluable psychological help.

CREATE A SITCOM

When Justin Halpern started tweeting about the funny things his 74-year-old father said, he quickly amassed 1.3million followers. He then adapted his Twitter page into a best-selling book and a CBS sitcom, starring William Shatner.

MY STORY: 'I TRIED TO USE FACEBOOK TO FIND MYSELF SOME FLATMATES'

Joe Ford, 23, Student

'I hate Facebook. I mean obviously I use it all the time just like everybody else but I do hate it. Mostly because it encourages me to do stupid things, like when I had a year abroad as part of my course at Uni and I decided to use Facebook to find housemates to live with out there for the year I was away. What a stupid idea. Of course everybody sounds nice and looks normal when all you can see is their birthday, profile picture and a few wall comments. Of course the fact they also have *24* and *Spooks* in their 'Favourite TV' section makes them look like they'd have decent taste and not be completely off your radar. And yet I shouldn't have trusted Facebook, and I shouldn't have attempted to judge somebody's character by what online groups they'd joined over the last year. Anyway I did, and it meant I spent three months of absolute hell, until I managed to jump ship, living with a guy who could quite possibly turn out to be the strangest French student in the world. I lived in absolute misery, and also filth, because another thing Facebook can't tell you is how much hair people manage to clog the drain up with after their average shower. Yuck!'

10 Things NOT to do on Social-networking Sites

1. TALK IN DETAIL ABOUT YOUR COMING HOLIDAY

Sure, your friends might be interested in knowing exactly when you're leaving and how long you'll be away, but so might a few passing opportunists…

2. USE FACEBOOK OR TWITTER OR MYSPACE AS AN ALTERNATIVE TO REGULAR EMAIL

Just because you're logged into your social-networking sites 24/7, doesn't mean to say everyone else will be too. Some people don't log onto their accounts from one week to the next. If you have something important to communicate, whether it's work or play, be on the safe side and do it via 'proper' channels.

3. ADD OLD FRIENDS, THEN IGNORE THEM

We've all done that thing where we get totally carried away by seeing a name that's a blast from the past, hastily send out a friend request and then belatedly realise we actually have nothing to say. Then six months later, we're taken by surprise when that person suddenly pops up with a weird comment, having totally forgotten we've added them.

4. ACCEPT FRIEND REQUESTS FROM PEOPLE YOU MEET ON HOLIDAY

You might be quite flattered when that couple you met on the last night of a fortnight's holiday in Greece suddenly want to be your Facebook friend. You might even think they might have some fun holiday photos to share. Don't be surprised when they remind you of that drunken invitation you issued for them to come and stay any time and told them 'mi casa es tu casa'. They might just have taken that literally.

5. SHARE PERSONAL DETAILS THAT YOU MIGHT HAVE USED IN YOUR PASSWORD

You might think it's fun to do that quiz where you make your porn name out of your first pet and your mother's maiden name, but it's not so much fun if that's either part of your password or your security question on one of your important accounts. Many websites that contain secure personal information require a password also and offer at least one password hint in case you forget. This might be what is the name of your first pet? What's your mother's maiden name? What's the name of the first street you lived on as a child. Including these details might typically go like this: You sign up for something like online banking and you get a login and password and then choose a

HELP! I'M A FACEBOOKAHOLIC

security question for when you forget your password. What's the name of your first pet? What's your mother's maiden name? What's the name of the first street you lived on? Any of these details might be a gift to an identity fraudster.

6. GIVE AWAY COMPANY INFORMATION

You wouldn't be that indiscreet. Would you? Actually, you'd be surprised how much we give away without even realising it. Sharing the news of your new promotion with your online friends, enthusing about the project you've been working on. All of these could count as Too Much Information as far as your bosses are concerned. Sharing work secrets is dangerous business, even on a nice day in the park. Sophos, a security software company, found that 63 per cent of companies were afraid of what their employees were choosing to share on social-networking sites.

7. UPDATE FACEBOOK PROFILE WHEN YOU'RE SUPPOSEDLY ILL

It's self-explanatory – and yet so common. People updating their social-networking sites with up-to-the-minute info on the wonderful things they're getting up to on their self-imposed 'duvet day'. You might not have friended your boss, but chances are news of your updates will reach him through friends or friends' of friends. That's why it's called a network.

8. WRITE ON A PUBLIC WALL WHAT REALLY SHOULD STAY PRIVATE

As a general rule of thumb, if it's not a public observation, keep it private. Nobody wants to know about your exciting weekend plans – except the people they involve directly. Putting it in an email or private message is sensible, posting it on your wall is showing off.

9. USE YOUR UPDATES TO SLAG SOMEONE OFF
Your social-networking page is not the right forum for trying to settle scores or win friends over to your side of an argument. Washing your dirty laundry online will rebound on you in the end, either when you make up with the other person and have to issue a public retraction or when they retaliate on their own pages.

10. GET YOUR FRIENDS INTO TROUBLE
You might well think the photo of your friend tied naked to the lamppost after a drunken night out is just the thing to brighten your network's news feeds. But he might not appreciate being tagged when the photo goes straight to his mum... or his boss... As a general rule, if you wouldn't want it to happen to you, don't do it to your friends.

Five Ways to Improve Your Facebook Pages

1. UPDATE YOUR PROFILE IMAGE
The Facebook profile image is the first thing people see when they reach your page. And the right picture says a thousand words. So think more carefully about your image and, if necessary, change it to make it as exciting and interesting as possible.

2. MAINTAIN AN UP-TO-DATE PROFILE
Ideally, change it every couple of weeks. The idea of the profile is to generate more interest. A static profile, untouched for months, means a life less than interesting.

3. EXPAND YOUR HORIZONS

The great thing about social-networking is it exists to extend your connections or friendships way beyond your real life circle of friends, school or workmates and family. One way to develop your network is to interact with the people you want to know, because you think they're interesting. Join groups that really interest you, rather than ones your friends are using, to find new people who share your interests and views.

4. DON'T BE TOO RETICENT

While you need to be diligent about cyberstalkers and the nature of the information you reveal, your interaction with existing friends should be as upbeat and entertaining as you can make it; write on their wall, make positive comments about pictures you really like, remember people's important dates, i.e. birthdays or anniversaries, things you normally do offline to maintain relationships or friendships.

5. USE STATUS UPDATES POSITIVELY AND CREATIVELY

Sometimes less is more. Developing traffic and interesting dialogue isn't always a question of sending out a nonstop stream of consciousness. For instance, asking lots and lots of questions and waiting for people to comment isn't always a good way to generate exciting responses. Nor is saying, 'I'm doing this or that', no matter how trivial it is. If you want to generate lively traffic, try asking one or two big questions, where you're really keen to know more. Or limit 'what I'm doing' to situations where it's something significant or fascinating to others. That way, you're making it more interesting for you and your friends.

6 Ways to Spot a Facebook Liar

1 One of the big signs of Facebook lying is where a person is constantly using less first person references: 'I came to London yesterday' is truthful. 'Got into London yesterday', dropping the first person singular, 'I', could be a giveaway.

2 People who are lying write more, they use more words. Studies have shown that online liars use a third more words than honest people. That's because they are really trying to convince you. And, of course, typing allows people to take more time over what they say than they can in face-to-face conversation: they've got the time to think about constructing their lies.

3 Are you changing the way you talk online? Research also shows that people who are being lied to online may change their own online language too: using the first person singular less, using more words and asking more questions. So if you do find yourself doing this on Facebook, it could be that by mimicking the other person's language you are already unconsciously aware that you're talking to a liar.

4 Learn how to trust your instincts. In any situation, ignoring your instincts can be risky. If you sense a warning sign and your gut reaction tells you 'this doesn't feel right' on Facebook, there's a good chance you're on the right track. So if you ask a question and you don't quite 'get' the answer, or think it sounds too vague, or over the top, be guided by your gut feeling. And back off.

5 Watch out for sentences that repeatedly involve the senses, as in 'I see','I'm hearing' or 'I feel so happy'; they're encouraging you to 'feel' too, and to open up. It's a very subtle way of exploiting your emotional response and drawing you in.

6 Ask the right questions. The more good questions you ask, the greater the chance of catching someone out in online lies. Try to get them to be precise. Who, why, when and where might not tell you everything, but they're valuable clues when you put them all together.

'Sorry mate. It's already taken.'

17
The Future of Social Networking

Twenty years ago, the Net to most people was something you caught fish in. Ten years ago, Facebook was just a twinkle in Mark Zuckerberg's teenage eye. The online world is nothing if not fast-moving. So will social-networking sites, now such a mainstay of modern-day life, stand the test of time? Or will they too be replaced in the coming years by the Next Big Technological Thing?

The jury is out on the future of social-networking. On the one hand, if you look historically there seems to be an inbuilt shelf-life for many sites. Friends Reunited, which at one point ruled the roost in terms of putting people in contact with others, has seen its dominance massively eroded. Similarly, AOL struggled to find a buyer for its one-time market-leading site, Bebo, in 2010, eventually selling for a small fraction of the price it paid just a couple of years before.

On the other hand, when you look at the way the all-time

giants of social-networking like Facebook and, to a lesser extent Twitter, have infiltrated into every corner of modern life, it's hard to envisage a time when they'll become obsolete. The question of whether Facebook is now 'too big to fail' is one which founder Mark Zuckerberg addressed at the All Things D conference in LA in June 2010, claiming that the Facebook brand is still very much in its infancy. 'Maybe I'm in denial. I really think we're just a lot closer to the beginning than the end,' he said. Zuckerberg also defended Facebook's much criticised privacy policies, predicting that the Facebook model of linking services and other websites to users' profiles will become widely adopted in years to come.

Zuckerberg is putting his money where his mouth is, contributing to a fund aimed at investing in social media start-ups, convinced that linking social-networking with everything from retailing to music to gaming is the way forward. Not only should you be able to go online to play games, download music, search key words, join internet groups – you should instantly be able to find out which other friends have done the same, what they thought and what their recommendations are.

FUTURE INNOVATION: THE SOCIAL MEDIA SOBRIETY TEST

Webroot's new plug-in 'The Social Media Sobriety Test' (www.socialmediasobrietytest.com) promises to save us from the humiliation of social-networking while drunk. If you're prone to posting while under the influence, simply nominate the times when you're most likely to transgress and you'll automatically have to go through some tests such as keeping the cursor inside a moving circle, failure in which will result in you being unable to share your drunken ramblings with the world.

The truth is though, that just as twenty-five years ago, no one could have predicted the speed with which social networking would become entrenched in the very fabric of our society, no one really knows how it will evolve over the years and decades to come. Technology is constantly evolving and, as it does, it changes the way we respond to and interact with one another.

Some people believe we will continue developing ever more complex ways of online inter-communication. Others are of the opinion we have reached technological saturation point and that the coming years will bring a backlash against the era of virtual social-networking, leading to a rejection of computers in favour of direct forms of personal communication. The days when parents and children would Facebook one another from different rooms within the same house are numbered, they predict.

Nobody can really be sure what the future holds. All we can really know is that for the here and now, social-networking occupies a massive place in our lives and, treated with respect and in moderation, it can be a tremendous force for good, linking communities and individuals and disseminating information and culture. Everyone is equal in social-networking. Everyone has a right to his or her place.

Social-networking has broken down barriers, of geography, of culture, of social status, and has put in place the building blocks for a more inclusive, more accessible, world.

What we do with those now is up to us.